BEYOND THE HORIZON

Glimpses into the Lives of Exceptional Leaders

by
Cam Danielson

With a Foreword by
Joseph M. Felser, PhD

Integral Publishers
Tucson, Arizona

Integral Publishers
4845 E. 2nd St.
Tucson, Arizona

Cover Design by QT Punque
Cover Photo collage: Mariia Sniegirova

ISBN: 978-1-4951-5915-2

CONTENTS:

Foreword

By Joseph M. Felser, PhD

I T WAS THE eminent contemporary moral philosopher, Alasdair MacIntyre, who long ago pointed out that our inherited cultural traditions
are essentially constituted by a continual, more or less continuous set
of arguments over what it means to be a member of that tradition. [1] To be
an American, say, or a philosopher, or a Jew, is to be engaged in an ongoing,
typically deeply contentious debate over what it means to be an American,
a philosopher, or a Jew. According to MacIntyre, traditions are not monolithic, timeless, static entities, preserved, as it were, in amber; rather, they
are dynamic processes of development, shaped and moved by conflicting
themes and ideas. They are, to put it in a single word, dialectical.

Such arguments may contain rival premises that embody and reflect
deeply conflicting, even incommensurable, claims to authority, knowledge, and truth; and thus yield quite different interpretations of reality. For
this very reason traditions are liable to lapse into chaos and incoherence
at any moment, and particularly at decisive junctures of change dubbed
by MacIntyre "epistemological crises," in which the growing awareness
of the possibility of multiple perspectives, and the inability to adjudicate
between them, becomes critical. The tradition may then either unravel
altogether, or else rise to the challenge of establishing a new cohesiveness
through a revolutionary self-reconstitution. It was just such episodes of
crisis in the discipline of physics, punctuated by the work of such creative
giants as Isaac Newton and Albert Einstein, that philosopher Thomas
Kuhn called "paradigm shifts" and made the subject of his epochal work,
The Structures of Scientific Revolutions (1962).

In other words, conflicts over basic questions of identity and meaning
are always at the heart of a cultural tradition, and will reach a fever pitch
of urgency at key turning points. A single tradition will yield different,
even opposing answers to fundamental questions concerning its own sig-

nificance, value, and purpose; and these answers will change, often radically, over time. The records of these shifts are the various, often mutually incompatible stories told in the present about the past: to wit, our histories. In other words, traditions have—or, to be more precise, are—rival histories. Ambiguity and uncertainty thus fertilize the creative roots of our common life just because conflict and change are at once endemic and unavoidable.

As MacIntyre himself would doubtless concur, what is true of traditions as a whole is likewise true of the individuals, as well as the institutions, that comprise them—and perhaps, if philosophers like G.W.F. Hegel and Heraclitus are to be believed, true of the very fabric of nature, the cosmos, and reality as such.

"Who am I? What is my purpose? What should I do?" From this vantage point, the self or "I" is not a single, simple entity, or a pure, unchanging substrate, but rather, a complex process driven and constituted by its inner conflicts and their complicated, ever-evolving dynamic, including a constantly shifting self-awareness and self-understanding. As we should have learned from C.G. Jung, we are all, in a sense, multiple personalities: a diverse, discordant family of selves engaged in an ongoing, more or less conscious, and often cacophonous inner dialogue.[2]

"Who are we? What is our true purpose? What should we do?" Similarly, any large organization—be it a government, corporation, political party, or academic institution—is not a monolithic entity possessing an unchanging identity with a single, permanent set of values, beliefs, and goals, or even an solitary locus of power. The congress and the president do not speak with one, harmonious voice; the AT&T of 2015 is not your great-grandfather's AT&T of 1885; the Democratic Party of Andrew and Lyndon Johnson were not the same parties; and a university faculty may clash with its own board of trustees on crucial matters of educational policy.

Heraclitus knew that these psychological, social, and cultural patterns have metaphysical roots. *"Panta rei,"* he declared: "Everything flows; nothing abides."[3] Fire and water, the two great polar opposites in nature, were his favored metaphors for the dynamism of the world-process. "It should be understood," he averred, "that war is the common condition, that strife is justice, and that all things come to pass through the compulsion of strife."[4] To think otherwise is sheer folly: "Homer was wrong in saying, 'Would that strife might perish from amongst gods and men'. For if that were to occur, then all things would cease to exist."[5] Stasis is death.

"As above, so below." Attributed to the legendary sage Hermes Trismegistus, this is the ancient mystical teaching of correspondences between the macrocosm, the great cosmos (order) of the universe, and the microcosm, or the little cosmos of the individual. The war of the gods as mirrored in the eye of humanity—or, alternately, the inward struggles of the human soul as projected outward upon the universal panorama—are related in the stories of our religious and spiritual traditions, or what Joseph Campbell dubbed "mythology," which he said is nothing more than the flight of the human imagination inspired by our own internal strife. "Myth" he opined, "is a manifestation in symbolic images, metaphorical images, of the energies within us, moved by the organs of the body, in conflict with each other. This organ wants this, that organ wants that: the brain is one of the organs."[6]

Myths, like the life-stories of traditions, cultures, institutions, and individuals, are thus also subject to conflicting interpretations, and have their own trajectory of development—their own history—punctuated by deep crises of self-questioning; crises that may lead to the revolutionary transformation or radical re-interpretation of a mythology, or even, in some instances, its utter demise. Thus the authors of the Upanishads revisioned the earlier Vedic gods in terms of an inward-turned mystical psychology; in the hands of a Siddhartha, Hinduism and Jainism was transformed into Buddhism; Saint Paul's blending of Judaism and the Mystery Cults gave us Christianity; and the worship of Zeus-Jupiter is no more.

* * *

The patterns of conflict, crisis and change, both in reality and in the stories we tell about it, are thus universal and ubiquitous. They are the basic leitmotifs sounded at every level of the universal symphony, from the heavenly music of the spheres on down to the different drumbeats by which each true individual marches.

The issue, therefore, is not whether we change, but rather, in the words of the author of the present work, Cam Danielson, how we confront the ever-present "challenge of change," especially "when the parameters of meaning that frame our understanding become elusive and ambiguous" -- that is to say, during those tricky, destabilizing episodes of epistemological crisis. "Too much change too quickly," and we are apt to lose our orientation, he observes, whereas "too much stasis over too long a period of time," and we are in danger of losing our energy. There must be a balance; and yet, there are also times when we cannot avoid such losses, either.

But this is not another dry, academic book about change; it is itself a book of change, the mere reading of which will promote the further creative evolution of the human spirit. That is because the book's author, while exceedingly conversant with the literatures of philosophy, depth psychology, business, and the classics (to name but a few areas of his expertise), is no mere armchair philosopher, think-tank futurist, or abstract theoretician. On the contrary, Cam is both a prime catalyst for, and direct experiencer of, the profound transformations of consciousness of which he so eloquently and thoughtfully writes in these pages.

The vineyards in which Cam labors are located in the fertile fields of the social mesocosm; that apparently solid, middle, mediating ground of our human institutions and their collective arrangements, where the microcosmic personal reality and experience of the particular individual meets up with—or, less charitably, bumps up against—the macrocosmic order of the universe at large.

Once upon a time, in the Middle Ages, the celestial hierarchy of the Father's Heavenly Kingdom was seamlessly incarnated in the earthly hierarchies of state, church, marriage, and guild, with their Absolute Monarchs, Infallible Popes, Kings of the Household, and Master Craftsmen. To establish harmony with the universal order, the individual had only to serve and obey (masculine) Leaders. The situation nowadays is, to put it mildly, a bit more complex for leaders and followers alike, given the ubiquity of democracy as a social model and the fierce leveling force of our cyber-technology. Even so, our institutions must serve the bridging function of bringing individuals together for common purposes within structures that serve as both mirrors of, and vehicles for, shared principles of order. The social mesocosm is still where the action is, where the rubber of the cosmic wheel meets the road of life.

Cam thus has his work cut out for him. His official, professional role as a director of executive and leadership development, training, and coaching programs has won him a formidable list of clients, including prestigious academic, corporate, and not-for-profit organizations. Unofficially, however, I have come to think of Cam as a contemporary incarnation of Hermes, the guide of souls and god of transitions and boundaries, inhabiting and traversing that fluid, creative borderland space betwixt and between worlds.

Indeed, the very concept of "in-betweenness," or what Cam refers to in these pages as "liminality" (from the Latin limen, or threshold), turns out to be one of the skeleton keys to unlock the mystery of change. "Liminality," he writes, "is a description of the transitional phase between different existential planes." Thus, there are liminal periods or phases of our lives, when we are in-between jobs, marriages, or homes; liminal stages of development, when, say, we are not children anymore, but not quite adults yet, either; liminal stages of thinking, when we have abandoned one system of values, beliefs, and purposes, but have not yet adopted another; and even liminal states of consciousness, such as the hypnagogic or hypnopompic areas that border sleeping and waking, and which, with the proper preparation, instruction, and guidance, may become gateways to the kinds of expanded forms of awareness long sought after by yogis and mystics.

What, then, is the proper attitude to take toward liminality? In Cam's view, one should welcome, invite, and even cultivate it. And I concur. A cardinal statement of this view may be found in Joseph Campbell's mythological commentary on Where the Two Came to Their Father, the Navaho war ceremonial re-told by Maud Oaks, based on the version given to her by the old medicine man, Jeff King.[7] In the story, the twin heroes, a warrior and a wizard, were miraculously conceived in a virgin birth when the Sun impregnated their mother, Changing Woman, by making its way across the sky. They are warned by Changing Woman not to venture too far from home, for there are monsters lurking around the house. But it is precisely to obtain weapons from their father, the Sun, in order to come to their mother's aid and slay those monsters that the boys seek to venture forth on their hero's quest.

"Don't go far from the house," Changing Woman instructs the twins. "You may go eastward, southward, and westward, but don't go north." As Campbell wryly observes: "Of course, they go north. How are you going to change the situation unless you break the rules? Her proscription is the call to [the hero's] adventure."[8]

Go North! We must therefore learn to make ourselves at home where there is no home, and courageously seek out the One Forbidden Thing ("Whatever you do, don't eat that fruit!" Yahweh warned Adam and Eve), and the phantom zones of reality. "Not unlike ships upon the sea," Cam writes, "these [courageous] individuals navigate their lives on the basis of a reality that lies beyond the horizon." A boundary, he suggests, should become "an invitation for further inquiry."

To allow oneself to be guided past all the known landmarks and familiar boundaries by an intangible, perhaps ineffable reality that can be intuitively sensed in a subtle way, yet not perceived by the crude physical senses or catalogued by the rational intellect, is, in Campbell's terms, to answer "the call of the hero."[9] It means becoming one of Colin Wilson's "Outsiders": individuals open to the experience of wonder—which none other than Plato himself declared to be the original source of all philosophical inquiry—and who, as a result, are driven to question themselves, their own dearest assumptions, and the received wisdom of their culture.[10]

Heroes and Outsiders do not love novelty for novelty's sake, change for the sake of change, however. They are not to be confused with aimless thrill-seekers or helter-skelter berserkers, just because the transformations produced by the strife of the cosmic push and pull are not random, chaotic, or meaningless. As Aristotle said, there is a creative intelligence in nature, which, implanted and expressed in each organism, propels it towards its own fullest development, mature completion, or wholeness. This impulse is what he called the *telos* (ancient Greek for "end, aim, purpose"). Or, as Black Elk succinctly explained to John Neihardt, "the Power of the World always works in circles, and everything tries to be round."[11]

In human beings, this instinctive, spontaneous drive to become well rounded or to cooperate with, what, following psychologist Karen Horney, Cam terms "the forces of spontaneous growth," is essentially the same process that Jung termed "individuation."[12] It is what Hermann Hesse called "self-realization;"[13] what Friedrich Nietzsche dubbed the "metamorphoses of the spirit;"[14] what William James identified as the nisus toward becoming "the More" that, in some important sense, we already are;[15] and what my friend and fellow philosopher, Michael Grosso, following the poet John Keats, has described as the project of "soulmaking."[16]

Simply put, the *telos* of strife is evolution—the evolution of consciousness. Everything tries to be round, as Black Elk said; and there is no final end to this effort: it is unceasing. To become fully aware of our own inner contradictions is to achieve or realize a level of consciousness that at once contains yet transcends our self-division and its tensions, thereby opening greater possibilities for choice, creativity, and freedom. As Cam declares, "Mindfulness is to view our lives as experiments in fulfilling our potential. We do strive for self-realization, and in that striving all data are friendly." This experimental ideal echoes Nietzsche, who urged us to find the courage to "become our own guinea pigs,"[17] as well as Hesse, who held each individual to be "a valuable, unique experiment on the part of nature."[18] To accept our own unique value and the project of living our lives as an open-ended experiment is the challenge of venturing "beyond the horizon."

* * *

I first encountered Cam's work several years ago, during my own border crossing adventure. I had decided to descend from my lofty theoretical perch, and the relative safety and comfort of my philosophical armchair, in order to undertake empirical fieldwork as a principal investigator in a research project. The aim of the project was to study the experiences of individuals who had attended programs at The Monroe Institute (TMI), in Faber, Virginia; programs that are designed to facilitate the individual's experience of various liminal states of consciousness.

What I discovered in the course of my own research was that Cam had paved the way for me with his own previous, extremely insightful study of

TMI program participants. This study is at the core of the present work and is one of its highlights. Subsequently I had the privilege and delight of meeting Cam in person, as well as the opportunity to occupy a spot on the same seminar program at the 2012 meeting of the Monroe Institute's Professional Division. I can therefore attest to the fact that the range, depth, intensity, and authenticity that is at once expressed and suggested in his writing is greatly amplified by his actual presence and presentation. Through our further conversations I have also come to appreciate his formidable skills as a listener, which is an especially important ability to those of us who may have forgotten how to listen to the voices of our own inner selves.

Another highlight of this book are the tidbits of Cam's own personal journey that are judiciously sprinkled throughout the discussion, as illustrations of his points and as guideposts for the reader. They are not merely interesting sidebars and welcome additions, however; on the contrary, they are the necessary accompaniments to his basic argument. For one of Cam's key insights is the extent to which the rigid, artificial division of the subjective and objective aspects of reality, knowledge, and self that is part and parcel of our modern scientific culture and its epistemology, has harmed us and hampered our efforts at seeking wholeness.

The knower ultimately cannot be separated from the known. This is implied in the Latin *experientia* ("to try and test for oneself"), which is the common source of both of our English words, "experience" and "experiment". Within the Newtonian-Cartesian paradigm, the meanings of these two terms diverged. But as Cam well understands, to accept the call of the new experimental life is to commit to bridging the gap between the "subjective" feelings of direct experience and the "objective" rational examination of data, between investigators and their subject matter, between observers and participants. This will be one of our greatest challenges.

NOTES

[1] Alasdair MacIntyre, "Epistemological Crises, Dramatic Narrative, and the Philosophy of Science," *The Monist*, Vol. 60, No. 4 (October, 1977), pp. 453-472. MacIntyre was my first and best teacher of philosophy. He served as my mentor, both as an undergraduate and later as a graduate student, when he stepped in to direct my dissertation while I was at The University of Chicago. In 1976, at Boston University, I took a seminar with him in which he was setting out the ideas that became the substance of his 1977 *Monist essay*. My discovery of philosophy triggered my own epistemological crisis, which in some sense is still unresolved.

[2] For an experiential exploration of Jung's ideas about multiplicity, see W. Brugh Joy, *Avalanche: Heretical Reflections on the Dark and the Light* (New York: Ballantine Books, 1990).

[3] Heraclitus, *The Cosmic Fragments*, in Jacob Needleman and David Appelbaum, eds. Real Philosophy: An Anthology of the Universal Search for Meaning (New York: Penguin/Arkana 1990), p. 173.

[4] *Ibid.*

[5] *Ibid.*

[6] Joseph Campbell with Bill Moyers, *The Power of Myth*, PBS Video Series, Part 3: "The Message of the Myth," accessed at *http://billmoyers.com/1988/05/30/joseph-campbell-power-myth-bill-moyers/* on 7/31/15.

[7] Jeff King and Maud Oakes, with commentary by Joseph Campbell, *Where the Two Came to Their Father: A Navaho War Ceremonial*, 3rd Ed. (Princeton: Princeton University Press, 1991). (Original work published 1943).

[8] Joseph Campbell, *Pathways to Bliss: Mythology and Personal Transformation*, ed. David Kudler (Novato, CA: New World Library, 2004), p. 127.

[9] Joseph Campbell, *The Hero with a Thousand Faces*, 2nd Ed. (Princeton: Princeton University Press, 1968). (Original work published 1949)

[10] Colin Wilson, *The Outsider* (Cambridge, Mass.: Riverside Press, 1956).

[11] John Neihardt, *Black Elk Speaks: Being the Life Story of a Holy Man of the Oglala Sioux* (Albany, NY: SUNY Press, 2008), p. 155.

[12] C. G. Jung, *The Integration of the Personality* (Oxford, England: Farrar & Rinehart, 1939).

[13] Hermann Hesse, *Demian: The Story of Emil Sinclair's Youth*, trans. M. Roloff and M. Lebeck (New York: Bantam, 1970).

[14] Friedrich Nietzsche, "On The Three Metamorphoses of the Spirit," from *Thus Spoke Zarathustra, Part I*, in *The Portable Nietzsche*, ed. and trans. Walter Kaufmann (New York: Penguin, 1954), pp. 137-140. (Original work published 1883)

[15] William James, *The Varieties of Religious Experience* (New York: Modern Library, 1938). (Original work published 1902)

[16] Michael Grosso, *Soulmaking: Uncommon Paths to Self-Understanding*, 2nd Ed. (Charlottesville, VA: Hampton Roads Publishing Co., 1997).

[17] Friedrich Nietzsche, *The Gay Science*, trans. Walter Kaufmann (New York: Vintage, 1974), p. 253. (Original work published 1882)

[18] Hesse, p. 4.

Preface

THE TRAIL OF writing that led to this book had many masters who I wanted to please, and tying the threads together wasn't easy. Before there was even a field called consciousness studies, I was wandering through literature, philosophy, psychology looking for what it meant to exist in more expanded states of awareness while fully present to the experiences of daily life. Eventually through my work in leadership development, I came to realize that the challenge I wanted to address is the interweaving of the contemplative and the active life. It is what I now call mindfulness, but twenty-five years ago it was not part of my world. However, to find examples of this extraordinary state and to learn what difference it makes to one's self and others led me to a number of explorers and pathfinders who I pay tribute to in this book.

In undertaking the research for this book, I started with a hypothesis about how people experience life differently at different stages in their lives. This point of view was first impressed upon me when reading the *Odyssey* at 18 and then again at 35. It felt like I was reading two very different books and made me reflect on why that was the case. What I noticed is how my personal lens on the stories of Odysseus' struggle to find his way home was less about the myriad of details of this epic of western culture and more about what was going on inside of me. The stories within stories that comprise the *Odyssey* became a means to objectify my inner state. In a similar vein, my approach to this book is to capture the stories of these exceptional people, distill a sense of their inner state, and draw out the implications for developing leaders and organizations.

However, there is a further reason for the approach I have taken in writing this book. I wish to invite the reader to experience his or her own inner state, through the stories of these people, and what that might say about what is yet possible for the world we live in and the communities and organizations we inhabit. To do that, I have used different writing styles to appeal to a wider range of readers and their personal preferences.

For some, the narrative structure of reading about people who have navigated the ups and downs of life will be most meaningful. For others, the data and quantitative analysis of their lives will be more interesting. Still for another set of readers, theory and model building about what potentially lies beyond the horizon will be most useful. Nevertheless, I will let the reader know when the shift becomes most pronounced so they can choose what they want to read in their own time.

In many ways this book began in 1994 when I made my first trip to The Monroe Institute (TMI). My interest in what Bob Monroe had started grew over the years through participation in different programs at the Institute. But the seeds of an idea that became a research project took shape in a meeting at TMI in the spring of 2006 with Laurie Monroe and Skip Atwater, then the President and Director of Research, respectively. The projected was launched in the fall of 2006 when Skip, who was by then the President of TMI, together with Darlene Miller, Director of Programs, helped create and distribute the initial communication to the relevant TMI alumni population. After the report of findings of the first phase of the study was released, Paul Rademacher, then the Executive Director of TMI, asked me to make a presentation in 2008 to the Professional Division of the Institute. The questions that emerged from that session led to the second phase of the study and ultimately the first half of this book.

I want to thank my colleague and friend, Tim Baldwin, Professor of Management at the Kelley School of Business, Indiana University who helped me frame the initial study I undertook with TMI. He introduced me to Curt Bonk, Professor of Education at Indiana University, who graciously allowed me to use his online survey tool in my research (and provided continuing assistance as I peppered him with questions in the analytical phase of the study). Tim also introduced me to one of his PhD students, Jason Pierce, now Professor of Management at Universidad Adolfo Ibañez, who undertook the statistical analysis of my findings.

I am also indebted to Bob Anderson, the developer of the leadership circle profile (an online leadership assessment instrument) who provided me with the data from the study he undertook with selected participants in the Executive MBA program at the University of Notre Dame and the extraordinary leader group he organized. The data made it possible to further illustrate the leadership profile of the individuals in the TMI study.

Finally, I want to thank my partner, colleague, friend, and wife, Pam Fuhrmann, for her loving support throughout the writing process and her editorial insights that made this a much better book.

Introduction

TO USE A modern cliché, we live in extraordinary times. But then that is what modernists believe about the times in which they exist; a period in history made exceptional by the endeavors or challenges they pursue, by the profound changes underway, and by the promise of what is yet possible. The more objective view says only history will know for sure, and yet, as philosopher, theologian, and novelist Soren Kierkegaard wrote, "Philosophy is perfectly right in saying that life must be understood backwards. But then one forgets the other clause – that it must be lived forwards" (JP 1: 1030). From this perspective, all times are extraordinary because they all require choices. The act itself, "to be or not to be," as Hamlet pondered, is that moment-to-moment experience of life that forever teeters on the brink of extinction. The evaluation of any moment in history (even this current moment which is now past) involves seeking less or seeking more life, and those, in my estimate, who choose to live as if more life is continually possible are the truly exceptional. They are the "yea sayers" in the face of life's difficulties, its disappointments, rude awakenings, and never-ending ups and downs. They are those living with adversity as a friend who provides the window beyond the status quo, helps remove the bias against the unfamiliar and turn unknowns into new areas of investigation. They are the ones who have every reason to be bitter but have chosen a different path.

This is the story of some of the exceptional people who populate our world. They come from all walks of life and play multiple roles from son/daughter, brother/sister, father/mother, partner, companion, friend, lover, teacher, student, professional, boss, employee, business owner, colleague, neighbor, citizen, volunteer, and leader. It isn't the multitude of roles but the consciousness with which they embrace them that begins to point to the diversity of their lives, internally and externally. I place the word leader at the end rather than at the beginning to enrich the notion of leadership. Too much has been written that puts the emphasis the other way around. Leadership has become the Holy Grail of corporations, administrations, and institutions, and because of this, has been separated from the other dimensions of life like a pinnacle. In that separation is the reason for the insufficiency that often lies behind the literature on leadership. Of course the cry for bold vision, courageous action, and a deft touch is needed, but that is always the case even when what is touted as bold, courageous, and sensitive really is not. A lack of perspective leads to a lack of inspiration. In times of uncertainty (and when will it ever be anything else), the need for inspiration before action becomes even greater as the level of anxiety rises. By default, shortsighted and uninspired actions are a result of shutting down and getting into our bunkers because we can't make sense of the environment in which we exist.

Opening oneself to the turbulence of the world with its multitude of voices and conflicting messages is what precedes inspiration. The mathematician and philosopher Alfred North Whitehead wrotethat "mankind is driven forward by dim apprehensions of things too obscure for its existing language" (qtd. in Pirsig 133). Beyond the known lies the unexplored and as more risks to adaptation arise (teetering on the brink of extinction), so increases the evolutionary impulse to transcend the pinnacle view of leadership through a focus on what wholeness means. Rather than viewing any particular orientation as a superior apprehension, the challenge that life presents is to create the space to simultaneously hold different operating logics and ways of making sense of things that often clash like fault lines. In this space much is risked, because it requires vulnerability in pursuit of mutuality, but much is possible in the reconciliation of differences through the emergence of successively more complex principles for organizing experience. The movement from dogmatic positions based on implicit assumptions to nonjudgmental awareness of those assumptions opens new horizons. The result can be a more expansive view of individual and collective identity, purpose, and capacity.

Coherently operating within the plurality of orientations that comprise the global landscape may be the greatest challenge of our times. The level of self-knowledge required to transcend existing assumptions and beliefs is the differentiation. To say this another way, if solutions tend to be limited to known ways of operating then problems tend to be defined to fit their solutions. A lack of curiosity about what we are not seeing, perceiving, or understanding hinders an openness to change and, as a result, a gap develops in effectively reconciling different values. For example, holding collective values that promote compliance (under the banner of "high ethical standards") and multiculturalism (under the banner of "valuing differences") sets up the potential for competing commitments and, thus, creates tension. Resolution is not found in a default position once discovered in a relevant situation of the past and now recited like a platitude because new situations will continually arise that challenge any previous precedent. Resolution is found in a way of functioning that continually recalibrates the interpretation and application of collective values – a much more complex undertaking that begins with the practice of testing one's own assumptions.

What I have observed about exceptional leaders is that they are first exceptional people. Their interior complexity is equal to the external complexity they face. The beguiling authenticity of their presence, sometimes described as sophistication, is an expansive, multi-dimensional state of awareness. The spectrum of consciousness they operate across is populated with multiple perspectives they recognize as aspects of themselves. They take the good with the bad, the creative with the destructive, the dynamic with the static, the imaginative with the concrete, the old with the new, the true with the false and call it all part of the life around them and the life within them. The perpetual unfolding of life, with its unfathomable depth of possibility, is the attitude they reflect in their willingness to examine what others describe as irrational. Curiosity is a factor, but more important is a willingness to face one's fears. For the people in these stories, the honesty by which they share their fears, traumas, and subsequent healing is startling. It takes courage to confront what has been unconscious, hidden, repressed, denied, rejected, hated, and feared, but no new thing is truly possible otherwise. Too often what is strange, different, and labeled with the tag "other" is shamed by behaviors of derision, dismissal, and exclusion. This is a reaction that shrinks the world, which C. G. Jung, the founder of analytic psychology, noted in saying that what is true of the world around us is true within ourselves:

The present day shows with appalling clarity how little able people are to let the other man's argument count, although this capacity is a fundamental and indispensable condition for any human community. Everyone who proposes to come to terms with himself must reckon with this basic problem. For to the degree that he does not admit the validity of the other person, he denies the "other" within himself the right to exist – and vice versa. The capacity for inner dialogue is a touchstone for outer objectivity (*CW* 8: 187).

What induces such deep introspection? What carries the day when things can and often do fall apart? As one woman in this study told me, "I knew I could become an incredible thief or a great person. I needed to find my own path to wholeness."

Collecting the stories captured here began when I was trying to understand why 17 individuals (who were a representative sample of more than 300 in a previous study I undertook) had a statistically significant difference in life satisfaction and self-efficacy relative to a control group. This required more than an online survey so I developed an interview protocol and assessment process to get closer to understanding this difference [Note: For those more inclined to data analysis, I have included a summary of the first phase of my research as Attachment 1. Similarly, a summary of the research protocol used in the second phase of the study is provided as Attachment 2]. To give a bit of a preview, a multi-rater, psychometric assessment indicates a leadership profile comparable to those in an extraordinary leader group (as detailed in Chapter 4). While members of this group cover a wide range of organizations—some in Fortune 500 companies, some in small businesses, some in non-profits, some in government agencies and the military—most now run their own business or professional services group. Interestingly, they are not easily defined by a specific career or area of expertise. Many have moved across several different fields of endeavor from theater to manufacturing, from opera to knowledge management, from teaching to physical therapy, from film making to information technology, from software development to wellness services, from sales to program management. A demographic profile of the group is provided in Attachment 3. Furthermore, the individuals interviewed have a mixed background in terms of their development as leaders. Not all have even held a formal leadership role. In fact, it would be a misrepresentation to say they all had notions of aspiring to leadership. What has earned them the leadership label is that they have been a source of inspiration to others under a variety of circumstances.

My access to these exceptional individuals may be explained as a researcher, but the welcome I received from them was also a result of my shared experience with the one thing common to all – we had separately participated in a range of programs at The Monroe Institute (TMI) over many years. The Institute, founded by Bob Monroe, is dedicated to consciousness research and education. Monroe was a radio executive in New York City who in the 1950s began to spontaneously move into an altered state of consciousness referred to as an out-of-body experience (OBE). He formed TMI to explore this phenomenon with the purpose of trying to regulate the OBE occurrence. What he developed went far beyond that objective. His efforts, together with those others who supported his research, led to development of the hemi-sync process and a series of residential programs initially launched in the late 1970s. Studies over the past 40 years in the fields of healthcare, education, and child and adult development have demonstrated the efficacy of the hemi-sync technology across a wide range of applications from enhanced concentration, creativity, physical healing and recovery to deep states of relaxation (Atwater 2). Ronald Russell, a scientist, teacher, and Robert Monroe's biographer, described the technology in the following way:

> Hemi-Sync (Hemispheric Synchronization) is an audio technology designed to produce in the listener whole-brain coherence; a state of consciousness defined when the EEG patterns of the two hemispheres of the brain are simultaneously equal in amplitude and frequency. It is based on two naturally occurring auditory phenomena: frequency following response and binaural beat stimulation. Listening closely to sounds of specific frequencies enables you to reproduce those frequencies in your own physiology. You can become

entrained to the state of awareness engendered by those frequencies (for example, they can alert you, focus your attention, relax you or send you to sleep) and with practice you can   learn to reproduce these states at will (2012).

While the study of consciousness has grown in popularity, a standard definition of consciousness has yet to emerge given the different episte-mological approaches (Danielson, 2012). Even the idea of empirical evidence is debated since starting assumptions differ. However, for those in this study, the examination of consciousness is linked to the philosophical questions of identity and purpose that go beyond who we are to what we are. This leads to a willingness to embrace unorthodox approaches to the exploration of consciousness if they prove effective in pursuit of the questions of being (our "whatness"). Therefore, interest in what can be described as esoteric ideas and anomalous phenomena are some of the things that made the participants in my study unusual, but it wasn't what made them exceptional. As already noted, curiosity was a factor, but it was how they integrated the lessons learned from their encounter with what was different, unfamiliar, or strange that had profound developmental consequences. Robert Kegan, a research psychologist at Harvard University, noted that one of the principles for thriving in a global world is to "resist tendencies to make 'right' or 'true' that which is merely familiar and 'wrong' or 'false' that which is only strange" (302). This involves a way of thinking or mental complexity that sets these leaders apart, and while intellectually I understand Kegan's concept of mental complexity, what it meant in reality was something I never expected.

I was privileged to have unfiltered access to the personal stories, dreams, and reflections of the participants in my study. The consequence for me was that I felt more like an interlocutor due to the unexpected level of disclosure rather than an investigator who had to work around the fringes of the conversation to tease out information. As a result, I have chosen not to reveal their identities but instead have given them pseudo names nor have I removed myself from the observations I am making. I have tried to represent a picture of what I heard and experienced with the same degree of honesty, fearlessness, and vulnerability they displayed. The dialogue or exchange between us is a movement between our inner and outer realities where the line between the participant and the observer remains fluid and ambiguous.

My time with these individuals left me reflecting on the role of leadership as I had been studying and practicing it and teaching and coaching others. What had been an emphasis on management, as taught in business schools, and competence in "business fundamentals," as determined by industry characteristics, is not sufficient for developing leadership consistent with the demands of a world of increasing complexity. In the final two chapters I make the case for a different way of practicing leadership that begins to address what I consider the greatest limitation facing organizations – relatively uninspired or shortsighted people who don't know what they are capable of. To make the connection more explicit, I have developed a case study of Dee Hock, founder and former chief executive officer (CEO) of VISA, who immersed himself in an ambiguous and dynamic context to define an organizational identity and purpose that was essentially unknown when Dee was given his charge. How he worked through the stages of exploration, integration, and implementation is a model illustrating a way of being representative of the participants in my study. Essentially, I am proposing that across the spectrum of information clarity and completeness exist realms of knowledge that require different states of mind or perceptual acuity. The ability to move in and out of these orientations reflects the agility of exceptional leaders in their interactions with others requisite to collective growth and development.

How collective development must be attended to, within the practice of leadership, is what I call soul work. A necessary ingredient is the daily challenges of life, which at an organizational level can very quickly turn competing commitments, values, and/or beliefs into a deadly spiral with implications affecting hundreds, thousands, or even tens of thousands of individuals. The magnitude is naturally of concern for any leader, and a search for more sophisticated methods of risk management is a worthy endeavor. However, when certainty becomes less stable, vulnerability increases in ways that mere analytics cannot address. While this conclusion my not be widely shared by more empirically inclined individuals, the global environment is changing economic methodologies and expectations in ways that require a different paradigm. As one international economist with a Brazilian bank shared with me:

> In the past, econometric models worked reasonably well in forecasting economic trends. However, today more guesswork is required because economic patterns of the past are not nearly as predictive of the future. The 2008 financial crisis has taught us this. We have to integrate more anecdotal data into our models, which means a greater reliance on questioning assumptions (Cherman).

"Guesswork" is another way of saying that imagination and intuition are required to expand the frame of reference. Is it any less valid if the result is in fact lifting the veil of assumptions that reinforce the familiar? Do we not hold, individually and collectively, possibilities that have yet to be envisioned? How do we imagine and integrate these possibilities in realizing our potential? Without doubt, there are horrific consequences to an "unthinking" or anti-intellectual movement that results in morals without mind. However, as I will argue, thinking is more than a cognitive process and we restrict our pathway to action, particularly in times of uncertainty, if we don't develop our capacity to use a wider spectrum of knowledge. This is the way of being that the ancients referred to as mindfulness or contemplation that I will explore throughout this book, first in the lives of these exceptional leaders, then in the paradigm of knowledge that represents the practice of leadership exemplified by Dee Hock, and finally in the work of soul-making as a collective endeavor to shift consciousness and thereby bring forth more life.

1

How It Began

A week before my first interview for this study I had the following dream: As I walk along a road through a forest, which is densely enclosed with thick foliage, I am surprised by the sudden appearance of a mythic figure that emerges out of the jungle of vines, trees, and shrubs. I have known of its existence, but have never seen one or ever believed I would. Much like the snow leopard, it is more legend than real because of the rarity of sightings.

It was a small, human-shaped being mounted on an odd animal that seemed to jump like a kangaroo through the undergrowth. The figure was enclosed in a garment that made me think of a Kachina doll. Its face was set inside a highly decorated hood that appeared carved out of wood. My astonishment was matched by hers and she immediately returned to the cover of the forest.

As I proceeded down the road in an amazed state of mind, I lost track of time until I came upon men along the road who were using long, tentacle-like whips to search the forest. The impression I got was an alien invasion in a deliberate effort to find these mythic creatures.

AT THE TIME of this dream I was uncertain of its portent. I had been traveling for a few weeks and had many things on my mind. So I wrote down the details in my journal without further reflection. It wasn't until after my first interview that the images of this dream came back to me.

I had included on my travel schedule several interviews for this study. The morning of my first interview I found myself noticeably quiet, as if conserving energy. I arrived at my destination on a beautiful day full of promise. Audrey was light as air, yet in the story she related, she was suffering deep

pain over a recent loss. Once seated in her living room, I began with an overview of the project and a review of the questions sent out in advance. With
little pomp, we were launched when I asked, "tell me about your parents:"

> My mother was of Italian origins from New York. My father was a
> mutt with Midwestern roots. The FBI recruited him soon after high
> school. He wanted to become a writer. My parents met at work, fell
> in love, got married. There were three kids, all girls. I was the old-
> est one. Mom suffered from postpartum depression for several years.
> She would put us to bed by 5:00 each evening and Dad would come
> home and come up to see us and we would tell stories. By my third
> Christmas, I was acting odd in front of the camera.

And just like that, I was quickly pulled into a life story that took me ever
deeper into its core. I could see the little girl playing on her magic carpet
with a neighbor boy and hear her describe how much she liked to read,
how she knew all the planets, and how she loved to play with her chem-
istry set. Then came the big day of change at the age of 11 when she had
to grow up much too fast with the birth of her fourth sister Linda, who
had a serious congenital heart defect, and with the emotional withdrawal
of her parents due to her mother's nervous compulsions and her father's
alcoholism. She now became the caretaker of her little sister with whom
she played through an imaginative world they created together. The strain
of those years showed on her face as she recounted how she dreamed of
running away from home. By high school she was out of touch with her
parents to such a degree that she was basically living on her own with all
the likely consequences that followed – sex, drugs, and depression. How
she managed to keep her grades up is anyone's guess, but she gave testi-
mony to the importance of her friends filling a vacuum in her life.

The maturing process of college laid the foundation for a successful career in business or so it seemed on the surface. Not far below darkness continued to haunt her and what followed were failed relationships, an abortion,
the death of close friends, depression and unemployment. But once again,
remarkably, she landed on her feet in a new organization with a new career

beckoning. This was a cycle that repeated itself over the first half of her life before she began a period about which she recounted a series of "road trips." A modern day version of the ritual undertaking of pilgrimages, she spent time at various centers of healing and self-exploration – Esalen, The Monroe Institute, the Barbara Brennen School of Healing. She was developing and honing her extrasensory capacity even as she struggled against those aspects of herself. Her journey included helping her youngest sister make her transition – "it was a beautiful death, we sang to her as she died." She is coming to accept herself in a much larger view of what that means – "we are creating all the time with our thought patterns, by forgiving, by remembering."

When I left I felt an incredible gift had been granted me. Audrey's energetic presence was much larger than the life story I had heard. The raw honesty about herself and her life, spoken with laughter and tears, surprised me. It was as if I had glimpsed a rare sighting of one who is living with knowledge of a larger presence that pervades her life. And then I remembered my dream of a week prior and felt the profoundness of what I was embarking upon. I had been given something I knew I had to protect even as I wanted to share it. The project, unknown to me until that moment, was to tell the story of a group of people whose lives are richly varied, filled with joy and sorrow, and yet consciously present to a spectrum of being that is mysterious in its vastness.

The Work of Telling Their Story

Each interview after that continued to reveal something new, something unexpected. The key to understanding the pattern I observed occurred in one of my final interviews when I heard a familiar sentiment expressed in Lyle's experience at TMI:

[It] got me outside of my box; got me outside of various traps, constructs, and concepts that had bogged me down. I simply got to a bigger state, a larger perspective... In fact, [these programs] for me are really about the unexpected. That is why I go back, for the unexpected.

This struck a chord with me so I probed a little deeper and asked what he meant:

> I am more conscious now. I get these little epiphanies such as "having a higher consciousness isn't about possessing yogic powers, but about being conscious on multiple levels, multiple dimensions and making conscious choices... It is being more aware, being more awake."

In that moment, I had my own little epiphany. I was in the presence of individuals who were striving to be conscious on multiple levels and, for that to happen, they were not merely open to learning, they expected the unexpected. Alive within an infinite universe that is also alive, they are yet distinctive in their ability to give voice to what they experience. The interchange of the two – the life around them and the life within them – is an ongoing process of creation, change, and growth. "Formation, Transformation / Eternal Mind's eternal recreation" is how Goethe captured it (79). It closely parallels what I understand Kegan and Lahey to mean when they use the term self-transforming mind (*Immunity to Change 19*).

Kegan and Lahey's model of adult development is built upon the Aristotelian precept that by nature we desire knowledge. Call it the other half of Goethe's vision of the eternal mind where our time-bound mind desires to know, to understand, and to make meaning of our experience. It is the human function we are given to develop upon our birth. Within this context, knowledge is a dynamic relationship between the knower and the known; the more awareness we have of the spectrum of our consciousness, the less unconscious we are of self-limiting concepts and beliefs (fears) and their reflexive conditioning of our responses to situations we encounter. It is an interactive process of widening perspective that views people "as active organizers of their experience... and psychological growth as the unself-conscious development of successively more complex principles for organizing experience" (Kegan, *In Over Our Heads 29*).

Major shifts in perspective leading to more nuanced understanding of ourselves and the world around us can be delineated in stages. Each stage is a shift in the level of consciousness in which a wider interest appears on one's life horizon. This emergent interest gives rise to new personal objectives, an urgency to acquire relevant competencies, and an appropriate sense of satisfaction in goal completion. But for what purpose or end is this quest for meaning, which I am framing as a desire to live more consciously? Karen Horney, an early pioneer in developmental psychology, defined the relationship between the knower and the known as a striving for self-realization. Arising out of what she referred to as a *morality of evolution*, the creative act that constitutes the dance of life is similarly a process of growth and change:

> This belief does not mean that man is essentially good – which would presuppose a given knowledge of what is good or bad. It means that man, by his very nature and of his own accord, strives toward self-realization, and that his set of values evolves from such striving. Apparently he cannot, for example, develop his full human potential unless he is truthful to himself; unless he is active and productive; unless he relates himself to others in the spirit of mutuality. Apparently he cannot grow if he indulges in a 'dark idolatry of self' (Shelley) and consistently attributes all his own shortcomings to the deficiencies of others.... We arrive thus at a *morality of evolution*, in which the criterion for what we cultivate or reject in ourselves lies in the question: is a particular attitude or drive inducive [sic] or obstructive to my human growth (15).

A philosophical foundation for a theory of development that becomes a psychological premise can be found in Hegel, who spoke of an Absolute as a construct for illustrating a cycle of becoming:

> The truth is the whole. The whole, however, is merely the essential nature reaching its completeness through the process of its own development. Of the Absolute it must be said that it is essentially a result, that only at the end is it what it is in very truth; and just in that consists its nature, which is to be actual, subject, or self-becoming, self-development (11).

In effect, no journey is a straight line and no stage of development is permanent. We can sustain our place on the rung of our evolutionary ladder to some degree by accommodating the changing landscape of our life with coping skills (acquiring the relevant competencies for well-adjusted functioning within a current context), but if we are curious enough or put ourselves in new situations, places, or jobs we increase the likelihood that we will eventually face the time when our world becomes too complex for our current frame of reference. In other words, incorporation of what is conducive or elimination of what is obstructive to our growth entails periods of transition or, more figuratively, periods of exile in some unfamiliar land. During these times we are restless, disoriented, anxious and rudderless. We become unformed (without clear identity) when the boundaries of an older way of life dissolve to give way to another orientation that is not yet clear. This is a trying time, but also one of opportunity as the limit of our self-knowledge gives way to questions of purpose and meaning.

Transformational growth entails a degree of uncertainty associated with our own completion or destiny. The eternal questions become more pressing at this time: Who am I? Why am I here, at this point in my life? Where am I going and how will I know? When we don't feel compelled to raise these questions we are under the spell of a current orientation, until the time arises when we are not. Then, once again, the questions we felt we had put to rest come back to haunt us. For example, our teenage years are memorable because of the great angst that underlies the change underway in our lives. In childhood, we were known for our narcissistic tendencies which gave us our endearing capacity to act unselfconsciously (e.g., spontaneously break out in song or dance in public) and our requirement for supervision to ensure that our impulsiveness did not harm others or ourselves. However, at some moment, we know we are no longer children, but are we yet adults? We certainly know more about how to behave in public than we did as a child, but is that all there is to being an adult?

This middle ground is fraught with ambiguity because no one quite knows how to treat us even as we express a desire to make our own decisions. If we are honest, we want to explore the world and ourself within it. But no matter how we try to explain what is changing in us, we are harangued, curtailed, and overruled by our parents. As we try to sneak around the rules we only find condemnation and more rules that make life unpleasant. If only our parents trusted us! But then, that is the point. As a teenager, we struggle with a crisis of identity that erupts out of our quest for autonomy. We want to take charge of our lives, but, to secure more independence, we must demonstrate an understanding of the needs of others through the way we exercise personal responsibility. Coming home from a party when we said we would, even if we are having a good time, means we can follow through on our commitments and acknowledge the support and help others have provided us. Without exact knowledge of when the shift occurs (call it the day our parents seemed to have gotten smarter), our world changes and our set of choices expand.

The trajectory of our life after we enter adulthood continues to be marked by shifts in how we experience ourselves and others. This process of development has only recently grown in acceptance among neurologists who had traditionally assumed that mental complexity did not undergo any significant change after late adolescence. "On the basis of thirty years of longitudinal research," according to Kegan and Lahey, the data show that "mental complexity tends to increase with age, throughout adulthood... [and] there is considerable variation within any age" (*Immunity to Change 13-14*).

Figure 1.1 – Age and Mental Complexity: The Revised View Today

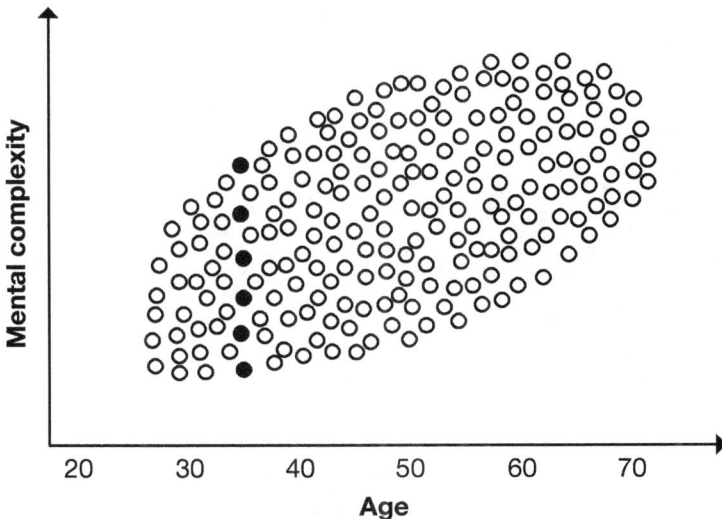

In Figure 1.1 from the research of Kegan and Lahey, the upward sloping cluster indicates mental complexity increasing with age (*Immunity to Change 14*). The solid black dots illustrate different levels of mental complexity for six individuals all close to 30 years of age. While there is an upward trend in the general development of mental capacity with age, there is still great variety among individuals. Some people may be operating at higher levels of mental complexity well before others reach those same levels, if they ever do.

The illustration in Figure 1.2 is the result of quantitative analysis of hundreds of transcripts of individuals interviewed and re-interviewed at several-year intervals by Kegan and Lahey and their colleagues (Immunity to Change 15). Figure 1.2 demonstrates:

- Qualitatively different, discernibly distinct levels exists that are not arbitrary, but represent different ways of knowing the world
- Development does not unfold continuously, but swings between periods of stability and periods of change
- The intervals between transformations to new levels get longer and longer
- Fewer and fewer people are at the higher plateaus

Figure 1.2 – The Trajectory of Mental Development in Adulthood

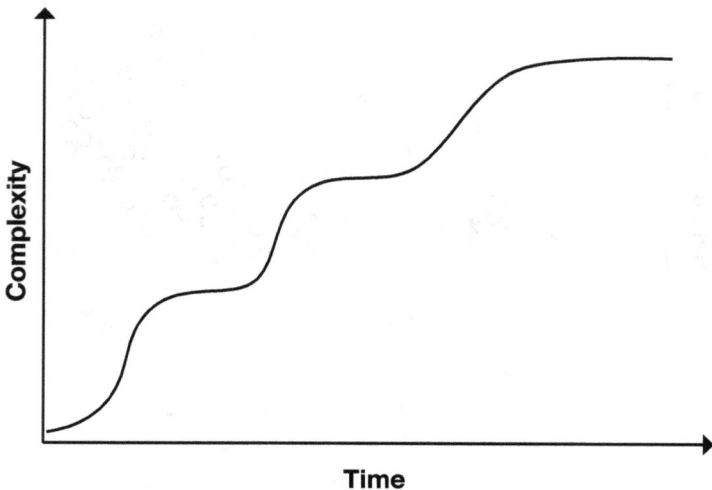

The three plateaus or stages that emerge from the data indicate different relationships between the knower and the known (call them epistemologies), each with a logic that provides a framework for extracting meaning from our experiences. At the earlier end of the spectrum, we are more concerned with how others see us – being perceived as competent, capable, and dependable - what Kegan and Lahey term the socialized mind (*Immunity to Change 17*). Here societal norms form the boundaries of the self and determine what is important to consider. In the middle stage, individuals have gained a notion of their purpose or reason for existence that extends beyond merely meeting the expectations of others. While feedback is always valuable, others' perceptions and guidance are now evaluated in terms of this purpose and its corresponding set of values (the self-authoring mind). The relevance of this stage to leadership lies in a person's ability to act even when aware of competing interests that cannot be resolved to everyone's satisfaction.

At the later end of the spectrum, perspective building beyond the limits of a single interpretation or understanding of self (and others) gives rise to a multi-dimensional, transpersonal orientation. Latent potential can manifest in many different visions of self with each vision comprising part of a whole (self-transforming mind). The leader at this stage of development can acquire alternative worldviews in the knowledge that no single perspective is sufficient to emergent thinking. Creating the space for mutual purpose (through finding unique solutions to unique situations) means having the ability to bridge paradox and the tension of opposites in a consciously competent way.

The individuals in this study are clearly influenced by their transpersonal orientation. How they attempt to gather perspective is the focus of their meaning making efforts, as a brief flavor of the language used by a few of the individuals indicates:

I am beyond the curiosity or interest in exploring the role of our minds in our experience of ourselves and others, to now having a firm conviction that we create the world around us with our thoughts. My work is like a prayer for me, whenever I face a new project and I don't know how to approach it I reach inside and wait for a visual to come to me. I am much more at peace with myself.

Olivia

Obviously the beliefs I hold do matter, but at what layer of consciousness do I hold these beliefs? How did I come to be here in this reality? Obviously my little self didn't choose this for my little self. That belief must have been held at the higher self level for this reality to be in the first place and for me to be here. It becomes difficult to sort through at what level I am holding the beliefs I use to create the reality I am experiencing - some would seem quite conscious like taking the first steps toward the sink.

Carl

I am feeling restless again. It is a periodic thing, and it tells me that there is something else I need at the stage I am in. This is the clearest sense of restlessness I have experienced, much less noise around it than in the past. In the past, I worked through my stages of restlessness by just sitting with it. The question now is not what's next, but what I want to make next.

Frank

I see my life as full of possibility. The question for me is can I open up to the possibilities? Can I see things in a different way? I am now walking my journey in a way I once only intellectually understood - staying in the moment. I can recognize when I have stepped out of the moment, but I know I have a choice of moving back into the moment.

Helen

I am much more aware of what is current around me, but it is like being in an open time book: touching past, present, future all at once. I can be present to others in this time and present to all time simultaneously. It is as if I am both a witness and a participant in the events around me. I can be in a doing mode and a meditative mode simultaneously.

Kenneth

I do not hold other people responsible for my happiness or fulfillment. I find that focusing on anger usually gets me stuck, so I experience it and move on. My guidance continues to remind me not to take everything so seriously.

Deborah

When I get into a state where fear enters, I can now let go. I am conscious of a quiet or a peace that is almost always present behind my ego.

Margaret

We operate across a spectrum of consciousness where every level has its work and we each have our purpose. You move to the work of the next level when the questions become nagging.

Peter

The me-ness that is inside is looking out of the eyes of my body. I have gotten most of my lessons through my body. Pain is no stranger to me. The way I can receive those messages now is very different. I once was very ambivalent about being here, in this body, but now I feel very complete.

Regina

I now vibrate at a higher level, and I can feel it, when I am in service to others.

Norris

In musing upon these different perspectives, three questions emerged for me that became the lenses or frames of reference for telling their stories:

1. What distinguishes their life journeys, particularly as it relates to what they value that helped them along the way?

2. What is their orientation for which the label self-transforming is but a threshold to a more expansive state of being?
3. How do others see them compared with my analysis?

The first question looks at a comparison of life experiences to explore similarities and differences and possible linkages to their current state of being. The second question is an exploration into a way of functioning that distinguishes who they are now. The outcome of this second question is five core tenets of their worldview or internal operating logic (their stage of development). Finally, with the introduction of a multi-rater psychometric assessment instrument, the third question is a comparison between how these individuals see themselves in terms of their effectiveness in interaction with others and how others who know them see them on the same dimensions. It is an opportunity to compare them, individually and collectively, to a database of more than 12,000 leaders assessed with this instrument and to make some specific comparisons with norm groups at different stages of development.

2

How Does the Spirit Move Across the Face of the Earth?

AMONG THE MANY experiences that entail a single lifetime which are the ones that provide a sense of someone's identity? It would be easy to say that every experience is a microcosm of the whole, but that only begs the question of what is the whole. And yet there are certain times and places where we know ourselves "without all of the baggage we have accumulated in this life" (Olivia). Those in this study experienced a number of points along their life journeys that were critical to self-knowledge, even if at the time the lesson wasn't clear. The interview process was autobiographical in nature giving the participants an opportunity to review and reconnect with life events that surfaced from their memories. What came out of this process was telling both for what it revealed about each individual and for the themes common to the development of who they are today.

Circumstances forced upon them a degree of introspection that catalyzed around the question, What do I do with my life? This is not a vocational question or even a philosophical one for these individuals. The question is based on what Colin Wilson termed the outsider's problem: "The outsider is not sure who he [or she] is. 'He has found an "I", but it is not his true "I". His [or her] main business is to find a way back to himself [or herself]" (147). In the lives portrayed here, an existential crisis occurs early, resulting in a division of self. By that I mean a shock to the participants' psychological make-up forcing a splitting or separation in the developing personality. The result is a protective persona that emerges as the "I" in interface with others. Alice Miller described this as the trauma of children who "develop in such a way that [they] reveal only what is expected of [them] and fuse so completely with what [they] reveal that one could scarcely have guessed how much more there is to [them]" (12). William Blake, an 18th century English poet, wrote of the childhood trauma that betrays our true heritage:

> They told me that the night & day were all that I could see;
> They told me that I had five senses to inclose me up,
> And they inclos'd my brain into a narrow circle,
> And sunk my heart into the Abyss, a red round globe hot burning,
> Till all from life I was obliterated and erased.
> (*Visions of the Daughters of Albion* 53-57)

While adaptation to the needs of others is a necessary step in the human journey toward wholeness, all children require a foundation "where a healthy self-feeling can gradually develop" (Miller 32). In the absence of such self-feeling, a child "cannot develop and differentiate 'his true self' because he is unable to live it" (Miller 12). What replaces "healthy self-feeling" is fear, distrust of others, and withdrawal as the following examples illustrate.

Elaine

Elaine was adopted as an infant by a couple who were as different as night and day. The father was a strong, out-going man from a poor, immigrant family who took on the world with gusto and gumption. He was going to be "a rags to riches" story, but it never materialized. Along the way he met a woman with strong southern roots and high society means. However, once they were married, they could not conceive children. It was a shameful thing for Elaine's mother to admit she was unable to bear children and the pain of her unworthiness was almost too much for her to endure. Even when her minister advised adoption, it became the lesser of two evils given the importance of her family tree and its bloodline. And yet Elaine's father encouraged adoption with the unbounded enthusiasm typical of his approach to life's challenges.

It was this context that as a child left Elaine deeply divided. Her father loved to tell her stories and "was always hugging me." She noted that he "had a golden energy and was wise beyond his education." However, it was a different experience with her mother. She was very distant, critical, and harsh in her treatment of her daughter. "My mother would never acknowledge my presence when we were in a room together and she could hardly stand to touch me." Her mother's treatment left deep wounds. Even though she found her father a source of strength and caring concern, she found she was forever trying to please her mother to no avail. It was primarily this experience that led her to say, "I had an unhappy childhood. I would look happy on the outside so as not to let anyone know."

Gwen

Gwen's father was an illegitimate child who became a successful "and well paid" scientist. She described him as "self-indulgent" and her mother as "frightened by the responsibility of having children." The result was an experience that she would only find out about years later. As an infant, while lying in her crib one winter day, her mother came in and opened the window before throwing water on her. It was a death penalty that was commuted when she returned to dry her off. Later as a school-age child, her father would beat her for wetting her bed.

An older couple up the road from where she grew up in the country became surrogate grandparents. They offered a much needed example of a loving connection, but her devoted attention made their grandchildren jealous. While returning home one day from a visit, their grandson accosted her. He stripped her and urinated on her. Between her parents and the neighbor kids (who basically comprised the older couples' grandchildren), she "was living in an emotionally barren place" and "retreated into my own mind."

Isaac

Isaac remembers the blitzkrieg and going to the bomb shelters as a small child. It frightened him badly. He was told to "put my fingers in my ears, and I won't hear the bombs." As he looks back on it, "I can see the seeds of my depression." He describes his family as "quite dysfunctional." His father was a drunk who beat his mother.

The family across the street was an important contrast for him. "They were so decent and well educated. They were a kind of oasis for me several hours a week for a number of years." However, this wasn't enough to make home life more tolerable or maybe the contrast was just too painful because he regularly plotted his escape. "I always wanted to get away on my own. I would slip away to go down to the river. I was a rather solitary fellow."

Kenneth

Kenneth doesn't remember seeing his father much because his father worked three jobs most of the time. When pressed, he noted that he has very few pleasant childhood memories. In fact he has lost blocks of time. "It was hell living around my parents. They were abusive. I literally spent chunks of time alone."

Growing up he was bullied quite a bit in his neighborhood and at school. He credits some of this to social class prejudice, but the result was the same – he got "beat up." He became fascinated with the idea of being "saved" as a child. Going to Sunday school was an important early experience. In many ways, his search for a relationship with "something higher than myself" was to find what was missing in his life.

***

While these may appear extreme examples, they are not atypical. The sense of separateness is a common experience. It is the mark of their outsider status. They could have succumbed to their alienation and looked for outlets to deaden the emptiness they felt. They could have become caught up in activities that proved their intelligence and intrinsic worth to others... and all did for varying lengths of time in their lives, but something continued to beckon them that could not be easily dismissed.

The burden of living with expectations that do not reflect the "true self" leads to a degree of self-imposed isolation. Solitude becomes a restorative, but more than that, it becomes a means for unconstrained imaginative endeavors. Through the doorway of their imagination comes relief in a freedom that does not depend on what others do or don't do. Yet, it is important to note the difference between grandiose fantasies and "the 'glimpse of power', of contact with some reality, awareness of a new area of [their] own consciousness, that came in a time of emotional stress" (Wilson 42). The former is merely an effort to compensate for living in "a state of noncommunication" with the true self and the latter is that moment when the cares and concerns of the personality fall away leaving the doors of perception cleansed (Miller 20). It is a time, as William Wordsworth wrote, recalling his own such experience,

> ... when meadow, grove,
> and stream,
> The earth, and every common sight,
> To me did seem
> Apparelled in celestial light,
> The glory and freshness of a dream.
> (*Ode: Intimations of Immortality 1-6*)

The natural world provides access to the limitlessness of being. In many ways, the natural world became these leaders alma mater whereby they experienced the life around them as wondrous and infinite. Here is where communication with their true self takes shape, outside the constraints of human society. Here is where they began to have a sense of the transcendent quality of life beyond the concerns of daily existence. In Native American traditions, this is referred to as stepping through the skin of the world (Martin 40-42).

Somewhere in the life of the historian Calvin Luther Martin the question of what it means to be a human being led him to indigenous peoples where a more fundamental question about the human relationship with nature arose. He noted as much in recalling the story of a Native American who had become a scholar, like himself, only to encounter his traditional ways in the crossroad brought about by his education:

> What is it to be an Indian? I shall tell you, said a young Iroquois, rising to his feet at a conference of native scholars at Princeton University in 1970 – I shall tell you what it means to me personally, he said. Once, just after graduating from college, he went fishing with his uncle. 'He's an old chief from home, and we are out there in a boat in the middle of the lake and talking about this and that.' Whereupon the uncle casually observed that, with that fancy degree and all, a young man must know who he is now. When the nephew matter-of-factly replied that he was who his name said he was, the older man was not impressed. 'Yeah. That's who you are, I guess.' Pause. 'Is that all?' Sensing he was being set up for something, the young man expertly traced his parentage on both sides and then ran back through his clan. 'I searched, and he chased me all over that boat for two hours. He wouldn't let me out. I was ready to swim. I was getting mad.'
>
> When he finally conceded, 'Well, who the hell am I, then?' the older man calmly replied, "'I think you know, but I will tell you. If you sit here, and look out right over there; look at that. The rocks; the way they are. The trees and the hills all around you. Right where you're on, it's water... You're just like that rock.' And I listened. He said, "You're the same as the water, this water.' I waited and listened again, as he said, 'You are the ridge, that ridge. You were here in the beginning. You're as strong as they are. As long as you believe in that... that's who you are. That's your mother, and that's you. Don't forget.'" "I never have" (34-35).

The degree of intimacy of the life around them to the life within them is as true for these individuals as it was for this Iroquois. Their circumstances may have differed, but their life journeys were similarly about reconnecting with something heartfelt through the call of nature.

Carl

Growing up on a farm can be a lonely existence. However, Carl never felt overly burdened by the fact that his sister was his only company through the first 10 years of his life. Being outdoors was more than enough of an adventure to keep his young mind fully engaged. "I liked being in the forest. I liked the peacefulness and the energy. I tended to always find space to myself."

He remembers jumping on a pile of sawdust from a logging camp when he was 4 only to find he was out-of-body. When he was 8 he recalls looking at a grove of trees and just sinking into them when all of a sudden, he shifted into the land of fairies. He would often find himself running through the forest. "It was easy to get into a meditative state while running."

In a statement that underlies his orientation, he recalls that, "the world seemed like a harsh place." To paraphrase Wordsworth, the world of getting and spending laid waste his powers. Maybe that explains why he never enjoyed going to the mall at the nearby town. "I got tired being around the people there."

Deborah

In the middle of the city where she was raised, Deborah spent "a lot of time in nature." She would scamper up and down the "mounds of earth on the lot next to my home." She loved the overgrown foliage. "The weeds felt like a jungle. It was magical for me." Until she was 6 years old, she "could fly and communicate with trees and other living things. I had lots of imaginary friends." Then she slipped on ice, slid down a hill, and was knocked unconscious. Things changed after this, "I could only remember flying."

But this didn't shut the door on her transcendent experiences with nature. Throughout her youth, she would have moments when she "felt a sense of grace and I would see the world differently. I called it the 'silver world' – seeing the world of nature as enwrapped in a living energy. At those times, everything was full of love and it felt very personal." When she was 14, during one of these moments in her "secret sacred park," she felt a "feminine presence that was very loving and full of grace. There was a voice that told me everything would be okay. These moments came to me as I seemed to need them."

Norris

Norris moved around a great deal as a child because of his father's job. His father worked all the time, but even then he "was not a play-with-the-kids kind of guy." Consequently, his memories of childhood are principally based on things he did with his friends and brothers. His "most vivid" childhood memories are from when he lived next to a forest. He and his friends built shelters, "we called them forts," and would spend hours in all seasons playing in them. In the summer, he caught frogs and tadpoles in the river or camped out under the stars. They were "experiences of freedom and exploration." One especially memorable event for him was riding bikes into the country to discover a horse farm where he and his friends went horseback riding. Like his other adventures, "it felt like I was very close to freedom to be outdoors where we could have reign over ourselves."

As he grew into manhood and watched his parents' marriage break up, he took his girlfriend to Sturgeon Bay where they shared the exhilaration of nature together. "As my parents broke up, my life came together."

Regina

As the only girl in a family with five boys, Regina should have been a queen among her siblings. However, she spent the first 18 months of her life in a hospital. By the time she did come "home," it didn't feel like home. "I was never really a part of the family." In her own words, she lived in a fantasy world. "I was a fairy-child, frail and light skinned. I had my spirit friends." She had an out-of-body experience quite early in her life. One day she was playing in a friend's garden and the next thing she knew she was at the top of the roof of the shed looking down on the garden. "I had a great sense of freedom even as it was quite scary."

From the age of 7 to 9, she was in and out of the hospital a great deal. However, it wasn't a difficult time for her because "my imaginative world is where I could be more active than in the real world with adults and older brothers." As she grew up, being outdoors was one of the real blessings of her life. She had many health issues that made her physical existence a constant reminder of her tenuous ties to this world. "My illnesses were a manifestation of my fairyness, my not fully being here-ness."

***

Moments of transcendent awareness are the bridge between realms of consciousness that can be entered through a secret garden, a favorite path in the forest, a quiet spot amid the grandeur of nature, or physical limitations. For these leaders, such moments were also formative experiences of their own sense of being alive and not just dealing with the anxiety of existence, however uncertain the implications for their futures. In my own case, I remember yearning for escape from the confines of my school. After the last bell of the day, I was always one of the first out the door and the road home turned quickly into a pathway to adventure:

Like drivers at the local stock car races, Keith, Curtis, and I ride aggressively across town on our bikes and soon reach the dusty country roads. The freedom of the open fields before us is exhilarating, and the anticipation of discovering new worlds only adds to our sense of excitement. Our adventure begins in earnest when we lean our bikes against the barbed wired fence that separates our Known world of straight lines, combed hair, and clean faces from the Unknown world of our imaginations.

We climb the fence leaving behind no-name identities and set foot on the other side as Explorers. The world around us takes on a look of strong contrasts - high mountains, deep rivers, and dense forests. It fills my senses as no small town collection of shops, schools, and houses ever could. I've crossed a threshold into a magical world where I and my friends can run with the buffalo among the tall grass of the prairie, then suddenly duck into a drainage pipe and emerge among the trees and vines of a tropical jungle.

While this innocent prelude to the adventures of my schoolboy years could be read from a romantic point of view, I prefer to see it as exposing an un-cherished truth. The imaginative re-creation of my world into a magical realm of mystery and adventure is memorable *because* of the contrasts that existed in my life, not in spite of them. Without a sense of "I," without unre-deemed self-consciousness, I would not have created this memory.

Societal demands do not abate and finding a place in the world con-tinues to create expectations. Being out of step with mainstream life is the new normal. The dissonance it creates is disorienting, particularly when efforts to build a life result in doubts, sadness, even continuing pain and suffering. For some, restlessness becomes a steadfast friend (and guide). For others, tragic shocks are frequent reminders of the chaos we cannot hide from.

Beatrice

Beatrice describes herself as someone who has "always had a yearning to talk about deep, profound, meaningful, true things." University was a disappointment because she was expecting "Athens and it wasn't. I was looking for wisdom, a meeting of minds." So she became an anthropolo-gist and then taught English as a second language. She wandered around barely scraping by in her first career before eventually landing a job in a major corporation on the East Coast. It was the same story, just a different setting, as she was hoping to find a way to create a more meaningful life.

Her wanderings have taken her through a number of organizations. Being a seeker has its own rewards, but financial success isn't necessarily one of them. "I have little concerns about how I am going to make a living. I have been poor most of my life. Self-preservation is my thing." Yet, the toll on her health has not been inconsequential. Dying at her desk was an impending doom in her mind. "I am more socially oriented and wanted to do a good job because of my friends and colleagues."

It is one of the paradoxes in her life, that given her orientation she has no interest in having an intimate relationship. "I think I am tailored not to have relationships even though I realize it would be a very good thing in terms of deeper healing. There is a part of me that would relax into life." When asked where her life was headed in her early adult years, she straightforwardly responded, "trying to get as far from my true self as possible and seeing if I can get back."

Olivia

Olivia dreamed of becoming a famous athlete. Physical activities were "the moments of my most natural experiences. I would go into a zone and could stay there for hours." However, when she went to university, she had a breakout experience in terms of her sexual awakening. "I had lots of relationships with different men." She ended up marrying one of them and took a job while he continued his education after they graduated. By no means was this just an effort to support her husband. She rose quickly in the company she had joined to eventually become a senior manager.

She eventually started and sold her own company in computer supplies. She felt "burned out" after just a few years and needed to do something else with her life. Moving to another city and starting a new career only led to another heartbreaking situation as her marriage fell apart and a new relationship started and ended badly. Her only guidance was that she needed to pay attention to her health. At the time, she was operating between two worlds, her private thoughts – "I spent a lot of time alone mentally, not physically" – and her public persona – "I got happiness and support from my social network."

Frank

Throughout high school Frank had wanderlust. He started hitch hiking eventually taking a total of six trips and going hundreds of miles from home. After that, university wasn't very exciting and he moved from one school to another before leaving school to work on the East Coast, then the West Coast, and eventually in Europe where he also studied theater. He returned to the U.S. and "closed out my theater interest." But this merely opened another door to another interest, this time in commercial design and manufacturing. Eventually he completed his degree and then later earned an MBA. Along the way he got married and had a family. "The marriage has been volatile with a fair amount of disagreement... we just have different objectives for our lives." His interests are as wide as his imagination and stir him deeply. Nearly 30 years ago, he created a list of important things to do in his life. "I review it once a year and create an annual plan."

When asked to describe his life, he has his own version of the song *It Was a Very Good Year*: "At 20 I experienced the world as this wonderful place to explore and discover. The world came to me. At 33 I felt like I was driving the bus. At 56 I was both the passenger and the driver of the bus, but my GPS was broken and I didn't know exactly where I was going."

***

How would these people integrate the different dimensions of themselves? What were they missing? So we return to the question of what is to be done with our lives as the central theme of the outsider. On the one hand, there are the practical requirements of life – responsibilities as a member of one's family, community, and society. On the other hand, there are the inspirational requirements of our true self – responsibilities to self-expression in stewarding the gifts we have been given. Similarly, there are those moments when the intensity of being alive is intoxicating with its freshness and, on the other hand, there are those moments of struggle with what is merely routine and mundane. The synthesis of these experiences is what wholeness requires, not a one-sided view of life. However, integration is never easy, because the result is a reversal of a logic that could not have been possible before – a mystery "beyond human solution," to quote John Henry Cardinal Newman (323). In Dostoevsky's The Brother's Karamazov, Mitya has lived in a completely self-absorbed manner most of his life. One day he falls asleep during a state of lethargy that arises out of the purposelessness of his life and has an astounding dream. He witnesses the human suffering of his country that leaves him wanting to cry, but more importantly, he feels:

> a tenderness such as he had never known before surging up in his heart... He wants to do something for them all so that the wee one [baby] will no longer cry, so that the blackened, dried-up mother of the wee one will not cry either... And his whole heart blazed up and turned towards some sort of light, and he wanted to live and live, to go on and on along some path, towards the new, beckoning light, and to hurry, hurry, right now, at once! (508)

As Wilson noted, "to escape the prison of his own self-regard, [Mitya]... discovers that he is in a world that is so full of misery that his only business is to love" (189).

A wake-up call shows up for the leaders in this study much like Mitya's dream, as the following story illustrates. There was a boy exceedingly blessed with intelligence, a handsome appearance, and a good heart. His life was enriched in the ways of his family and a community proud of his future promise and opportunities. As this boy grew toward manhood, his thoughts turned more and more to what lay beyond the horizon, what adventures would be his, and the greatness he would achieve. Naturally, he had dreams like other boys, but people in his community took him more seriously. If he dreamed of becoming a scientist and discovering new wonders or the leader of an expedition exploring unseen worlds, those who knew him would nod their heads approvingly and murmur, "You can make it happen."

In his young adulthood, he saw his life in terms of a quest and felt a kinship to those knights of long ago whose adventures filled his imagination as a boy. There was much to compare for his life was indeed adventuresome, but with each new accomplishment he grew more and more restless. He had become driven to conquer every challenge, attack every problem he encountered. However, each success felt as if he had scaled a mountaintop only to find another mountain that beckoned him. Metaphorically, he was in search of that highest point from which he could see unveiled the secrets of the universe. He knew there was an ultimate truth, a Holy Grail, and his feelings of incompleteness focused on possessing it. Over the years, he became a powerful and influential man, but increasingly distant from others, losing many old friends and making no new ones. Then one day, he found himself bitterly alone as he began to doubt if he would ever come to the end of his quest. He fell into despair and drifted without the strength of his former days guiding him. He wandered aimlessly until he lost all track of time and place. Days melted into weeks, and weeks into months. Nothing seemed to matter; nothing possessed him until he was totally submerged in emptiness.

He came to himself at a spot where he observed another man dancing alone. He heard no music, only the wind through the trees. He saw no one else, only the setting sun on the distant horizon. He felt himself bathed in the coolness of approaching night and wondered aloud why the man was dancing. The dancer stopped and called out to the despairing man to come join him. Immediately he was jolted out of his dream-like state with feelings of uncomfortable exposure, awkward self-consciousness, and a need for distance supplanting any wonder he had felt at the sight of the dancer. As he began to leave, dismissing the offer as that of a fool, he heard the dancer begin to speak, and as he listened, he stopped, turned, and drank deeply his words. For a moment, he felt transfigured, drinking from a cup he recognized as the Grail. In his surprise, he looked at the dancer and asked, "Where did you, whom I had dismissed as but a fool, find what I in my best efforts could not?"

The dancer's response was simply, "You were thirsty, and I sought to give you refreshment." What words could have such power to account for this conversion from despair... different words for different people at different points in their lives. There is such a thing as the fullness of time when something is understood that just couldn't have been understood before. Understanding is not merely the accumulation of more and more information leading to a rational assessment of our situation, rather it is that moment when seemingly unrelated thoughts, voices, and actions come together to reveal the image of a dance behind the mundane, the chaotic, and the uninspired life of "a state of noncommunication" with one's true self. For our hero, the call to the dance began with these words:

> have patience with everything unresolved in your heart
> and try to love the questions themselves
> as if they were locked rooms or books
> written in a very foreign language.
> Don't search for the answers,
> which could not be given to you now,
> because you would not be able to live them.
> And the point is, to live everything.
> Live the questions now.
> Perhaps then, some day far in the future,
> you will gradually, without even noticing it,
> live your way into the answer.
> (Rilke, *Letters to a Young Poet* 34-35)

In a similar way, the leaders in this study found themselves "living their questions" that led them to stories, dreams, and signs of various kinds pointing beyond their horizons.

Helen

For Helen, undergoing therapy with her children "helped me become a stronger person, which may have contributed to the demise of my marriage. I had stopped trying to please everyone." As simple as that sounds, it was anything but easy. An objective of the therapeutic process was to spend time on things she wanted to do. "The hardest part was figuring out what that was because I didn't know what I wanted." It was quite a statement from someone who had been an honor student and eventually completed her PhD. As she noted, "the overriding theme of my education was the creative thinking aspect I experienced in myself... I loved making connections between things, ideas, categories."

After her separation from her husband, she moved to another city on her own. She took up her professional work where she has been "blessed with some wonderful mentors. It has seemed that every turn in the road of my professional journey, the next teacher was there for me." The same could be said of her personal life. It wasn't long before a colleague she had only recently met introduced her to The Monroe Institute. "There were huge changes occurring in my life leading up to these synchronistic events. Here was something that came my way which I can say I have been looking for all my life, but didn't know I was until it showed up."

In her first program, she had "a quantum shift in my perception of myself. I realized that so much of the love I have for my work and for my kids is a result of working out of a whole brain where I can use my intuitive nature." It became an intuitive knowing in itself that "showed up as a spider web – an image of everything connected; disturb one part and it affects it all."

Lyle

Lyle has made his way in the world through a variety of interests that have never seemed to jell very well together. The result has been a significant divide between his private life and his career. "My colleagues at work do not know about my esoteric interests. I have not met too many people like myself who go out on a limb like I tend to do." His second wife shared his interests in hermetic philosophy. This eventually led them "into meditation which became a very serious practice for us 4-5 years into our marriage." His "development has been pretty amazing" over the course of attending programs at TMI. "While I thought I was reinventing myself many years ago prior to attending TMI, I have reinvented myself several times since. Meditation was the foundation building work, learning to be more calm and centered. TMI is more pro-active. It is less about learning to be calm than it is about self-empowerment, self-discovery."

The change is evident in his assessment of his relationship with others. "I am less co-dependent. I come up to the table now. I know this because I am more detached in a healthy way. It surprises me sometimes to see how I am dealing with events in my life that would have been too emotionally intense for me just a couple of years ago." His bottom line, "I have a sense of acceleration in alignment with my higher self."

Margaret

Margaret wanted to go to the Olympics as a horse rider, but "I didn't get a chance because I broke my back in a fall from a horse." As the memory stirs her she notes how shaky she feels adding, "I could have been a paraplegic." While it was three years before she was pain free, after only 10 weeks of recuperation from her injury she was back in the saddle.

Ever since she was a child, she could communicate with animals. One of the lessons she learned early was that "animals are very open and people put up screens." Throughout her life, developing the level of trust and openness with people that she shares with animals has been a struggle. She did lots of transactional analysis work throughout the mental decline and eventual suicide of her first husband. It taught her to "avoid people who play games."

She came to TMI "due to instructions from my inner guidance I received during master Reiki training." From the start, each program she attended allowed her to step outside and "let go" of the fear that enters through her empathic abilities. The epiphany occurred when "my heart opened and I felt myself as pure, unconditional love. I was all that is." One result, which she shared with a smile, is that prior to TMI, "I could not listen to the horse and my client at the same time. I had to phase out from one or the other and it took time to go back and forth. Now I can stay in different phases of consciousness at the same time."

Peter

A rambunctious child, Peter could not sit still very long and remain focused. This created a number of challenges for him. "I did a lot to piss people off." His parents finally got an assessment from a psychologist, whose conclusion was remarkably consistent with what everyone already knew. "Get this boy into the woods," is what the psychologist told his parents. "He has a real aptitude for some outdoor career and is not suited for office work." While there were many different paths towards this goal, circumstances weighed in and he eventually found himself in the military. "I thrived in the bush. My intuition kicked in and I could tell if and where there was a breakdown in the communication line around our camp perimeter. I would have an impression coming out of a field of consciousness that guided me, if I chose to."

While still a teenager he had seen a book his father was reading called *Journeys Out of the Body*. He tried to read it himself, but "it scared me so much I couldn't finish it." Many years later he was in an old bookstore when he found another of Bob Monroe's books, *Far Journeys*. This made a different impression on him and his interest grew. By the time he came to his first program at TMI, he was very sick though he didn't know it. Plus, "I was getting desperate. I was not getting anywhere in my own agenda of answering questions... I was not doing the important stuff yet." Six months later, he was diagnosed with leukemia.

He spent the time preparing for leukemia treatment using hemi-sync and as much as possible while in the hospital. "I was conscious, but I was gone." When they let his wife sleep in his hospital room, he knew he was doing poorly in his treatment. "I knew that it meant I was in bad shape." One evening while he was sleeping, his wife noticed a blue beam of light with laser intensity enter the room from the wall. It moved to align itself with Peter as if it were guided and entered his body from the soles of feet and exited through the top of his head. The next day he began to improve and soon he was in remission. In the succeeding years, he has had no relapse.

When asked what happened to his agenda of "answering questions," he shared a few thoughts. "While I began trusting my inner voice early on the job, I only became conscious of an inner knowing after TMI. There is a structure and purpose here and it is under control. You want to do more good than harm, but you don't worry about being cheated. The good thing about death is that you are not going to die; you know where you are going."

***

It is important to note that TMI is not a "vision" factory. Participating in the hemi-sync process does not imply that all you have to do is lie or sit passively and something will happen. TMI is a catalyst for those I have described as outsiders, individuals who are not content to seek stability through conformity within their social context. They are self-transforming because they live under the aspect of their higher self, what Wilson refered to as "the Will to more life" or Jung refered to as "the drive towards individuation." They are living on the edge of any collective identity as scouts or guides in the work of extending the boundaries of consciousness. These individuals achieve a much closer proximity and attentiveness to their conscious and unconscious states of mind, to action and stillness, to being the participant and the observer, to the boundary between what is known and unknown. This is why returning to TMI for the participants in this study is like returning home after being adrift among people sleep-walking through life encumbered with project plans, performance reviews, endless meetings, and unsustainable schedules.

Even Jung felt the stigma of being an outcast when, in his autobiography, he reflected on the time he was caught in the throes of uncertainty about how to proceed with his own career:

> The consequence of my resolve, and my involvement with things which neither I nor anyone else could understand was an extreme loneliness. I was going about laden with thoughts of which I could speak to no one: they would have been misunderstood. I felt the gulf between the external world and the interior world of images in its most painful form. I could not yet see that interaction of both worlds which I now understand. I saw only an irreconcilable contraction between "inner" and "outer" (*Memories, Dreams, Reflections* 194).

The goal of integration or wholeness between the inner and the outer is a journey whose destination, on a mythic level, lies beyond the rainbow or behind the veil or through the looking glass. It is not unlike the goal of mystics, philosophers, and poets of previous eras who wanted to form communities, academies, or schools. The poet W.B. Yeats created plans for a brotherhood of poets who would live in The Castle on the Rock at Lough Kay in Roscommon, Ireland:

> I had an unshakeable conviction, arising how or whence I cannot tell, that invisible gates would open, as they opened for Blake, as they opened for Swedenborg, as they opened for Boehme, and that this philosophy would find its manuals of devotion in all imaginative literature (169-170).

To be fair, TMI has never been the only means, or even the first means, for doing the deep inner work requisite to communication with the true self. Among these individuals, there has been and continues to be quite an array of developmental activities from psychotherapy, physical training, outdoor adventures, meditative retreats, educational workshops and excursions to spiritual communities. Attachment 4 gives an overview of the various references.

How these leaders happened to start down the path of integration is never quite as simple or straightforward as circumstances may imply. The synchronicity behind the events of their lives is part of the profundity of their stories. An inner drive to self-realization in choosing more life rather than holding on to their excuses, their victimization, or other self-limiting beliefs is what ultimately leads the outsider from the path of exile. Transformation begins through encounters with what Jung called "the life instinct... [which] comes to us from within" (*Memories, Dreams, Reflections* 349). Over and over in these interviews it became evident that the role of doing our inner work is "cleansing the doors of perception." And the result is that "everything appears as it is, infinite" (Blake, *Marriage of Heaven & Hell* 44).

3

What's on the Other Side
of the Rainbow?

A STORY BY CICERO tells about the grandson of a famous Roman military leader who had a dream in which his grandfather gave him a vision of life on earth from the far reaches of the heavens:

> And as I looked on every side I saw things transcendently glorious and wonderful. There were stars which we never see from the earth, and all were vast beyond what we have ever imagined. The least was that farthest from heaven and nearest the earth which shone with a borrowed light. The starry spheres were much larger than the earth; the earth itself looked so small as to make me ashamed of our empire, which was a mere point on its surface.

> As I gazed more intently on earth, [my grandfather] said: "How long will your mind be fixed on the ground? Do you not see what lofty regions you have entered? These are the nine circles, or rather spheres, by which all things are held together (164).

The comprehension of this vision and the interconnections underlying his world left the dreamer amazed (which continued upon awakening even without recall of the insights he had received). He had never conceived of trying to understand his world by looking back on the earth. This shifted everything for him in terms of how he thought of himself and where he came from. No longer was he limited to the boundaries of what had been his known reality embedded on the surface of the planet.

What made Cicero's story more than merely a part of his larger work on governance (entitled *De re publica*) is the discussion on the soul in relation to the body. Consciousness is not confined to physically imposed limitations and, as a consequence, the question of who and what we are is less easily defined. As the dreamer witnesses, his grandfather makes explicit the distinction:

> Do not consider yourself, but your body, to be mortal. For you are not the being which this corporeal figure evinces; but the soul of every man is the man, and not that form which may be delineated with a finger (168).

The argument that Cicero pursues is that the physical realm is but one dimension of reality and the essence of each person is more than what is defined by the body. He takes the position that humankind is linked, via their souls, to a non-physical realm. This left the young dreamer with more to explore than he had considered.

This centuries-old story was a constant backdrop in my interviews. Each participant struck me as a modern-day astronaut who was sharing metaphorically experiences of looking back on the earth. On more than one occasion I was reminded of a Shakespearean sonnet on the nature of love, which he described as "the star to every wandering bark,/Whose worth's unknown, although his height be taken" (116: 7-8). Not unlike ships on the sea, these individuals navigate their lives on the basis of a reality that lies beyond the horizon. Rather than orienting themselves in terms of their identity and purpose on the surface of their lives, generally or specifically, they find their location – their sense of place and direction – in relationship to the unfathomable depth and infinite dimensions of love.

There are a number of implications to be drawn from a self-orientation based on a transpersonal perspective. From my interviews I can capture the following elements:

1. Engagement of Multiple Intelligences – development of multiple forms of expression including music, art, and physical movement (dance, athletics, body work) to supplement abstract reasoning as a way of knowing.
2. Anticipation of Liminal States – being in transition on a more frequent basis and the increased interest in the white space or the unformed dimension of possibility that exists between two or more existential planes.
3. Relationship with Inner Guidance – being present to an interior silence or transpersonal awareness while simultaneously interacting in the world.
4. Playfulness toward Life – being open to the dynamic forces of change without succumbing to socially accepted beliefs, biases, or assumptions regarding their meaning.
5. Compassion for Oneself and Others – the essence behind the instinctual needs of human existence which shows up in a qualitative shift in regard to self and others.

These are not competencies, in traditional leadership language, but rather characterizations or descriptions of how I see these leaders through the stories they shared and their dialogue and interaction with me. While the descriptions create a composite that is notable in illustrating what I find unique and common among them, it is not my intention to be prescriptive. There are probably a thousand different ways to describe them and all would fall short of the fullness of who they are. Rather these descriptions are thresholds that invite us to step across into their lives.

Engagement of Multiple Intelligences

What constitutes intelligence is often debated; however, the importance placed upon intelligence as an indicator of human distinction is not. The usual tribute to human existence is the development of language, technology, art, architecture, and organization evident in what is described as civilization. Yet the question remains: What is the nature of intelligence that makes these developments possible, that "imparts truth to the known and the power of knowing to the knower" (Plato, *Republic* VI: 508e)? What Socrates goes on to note in making the link between the knower and the known is the role of insight – quite literally an inner light. While definitions of intelligence vary, the root meaning of the word is "to understand." However, understanding begins with acknowledgement of self-limiting perceptions that can proscribe access to insight. To revel in the question rather than possess an answer is to proceed from the known into the unknown with the realization, according to Werner Heisenberg, a Nobel Prize physicist, that "we may have to learn at the same time a new meaning of the word understanding" (201). What Heisenberg came to realize in the course of developing a scientific principle based on relationships of uncertainty is that the wider one's embrace of the objects of knowledge – the "things" that comprise our notion of reality – the more the results challenge underlying assumptions about the solidness of those "things." Such a paradox is particularly relevant to the leaders in my study in attempting to understand their transpersonal orientation.

Heisenberg was a classically trained physicist who, along with several other scientists in the early half of the 20th century, encountered very disturbing evidence that seemed to indicate an irrationality operating at the smallest levels of nature. What he discovered was that subatomic particles (e.g. electrons) exhibit contradictory behaviors depending on the type of experiment conducted. Heisenberg described his personal challenge:

> Can nature possibly be as absurd as it seemed to us in these atomic experiments?... The assumption that this was actually true led to limitations in the use of those concepts that had been the basis of classical physics since Newton... One had learned that the old concepts fit nature only inaccurately (42-43).

He had come to an epistemological shift with regard to the nature of knowledge. Rather than beginning with the thesis that scientific objectivity is possible in the observation of natural phenomena, Heisenberg's principle implies that it is limited to that part of nature that allows it. There are parameters to what can be discovered by use of the principles of classical science, and the limiting factor is the unique role each observer plays in interaction with what is observed. "In this way quantum theory reminds us, as [Niels] Bohr has put it, of the old wisdom that when searching for harmony in life one must never forget that in the drama of existence we are ourselves both players and spectators" (Heisenberg 58).

The search for meaning may be the driving force of human existence, but as Heisenberg noted, our role in that journey is more instrumental than we know to the insight we receive. Often the questions we have are a matter of survival; an attempt to deal with pain and suffering through an inquiry into why things happen the way they do. In these situations there is real urgency in the effort, but the passion or energy associated with this search for answers is not enough to comprehend what is meant by intelligence. Passion is necessary, but it is not sufficient. There are the dimensions of curiosity and imagination that when coupled with passion creates the condition for insight. For those gifted with the irreverent quality of exploration for its own sake, questions are merely the means for taking the next step into the unknown.

Across the board, curiosity and imagination were nurtured early in the lives of the participants in my study. One of the first common data points to emerge from the interviews was the number of individuals who spoke about their early memories of reading, which is a subset of their more general comments regarding the importance of reading in their lives. Reading, as they described it, is like stepping into a transporter room that beams them into other worlds. So it would come as no surprise that behind the value of reading is a rich imaginative life which took root in many different activities:

> I played a lot of games with my sister. I remember playing Operator. I also remember a boy in Russia who I climbed trees with. I didn't have many friends so I would spend time alone – mentally, not physically. I lived in a city and would spend time observing others. While I didn't have imaginary friends or fantasies, I do remember thinking "Here I am 4 years old and it is the right age." I had more philosophical thoughts about things.
>
> *Olivia*

As a child I could see things out of the corner of my eye and believed I was seeing into other dimensions.

Frank

I was really good at daydreaming. I liked to role play... Because of my father's work [a historian who recreated live representations of American pioneer life], I lived in a fantasy world. Life was all about going out to have adventures.

Beatrice

I liked climbing trees – it was quiet and it was in nature. I stuffed a lot of things inside of me and then I would read books and go climb trees to deal with it... If I ever got bored, I could always daydream.

Helen

I spent a lot of time alone. I liked to read and draw. My earliest memory was drawing rockets to Pluto. I was reading mostly non-fiction as a child. I liked books on airplanes and astronomy. I also played cops and robbers/cowboys and Indians with the kids in the neighborhood. We didn't have many toys so we had to be pretty imaginative. I would just play anything that was make-believe.

Lyle

I usually played games with adults. I began playing chess at 3 or 4. I spent a lot of time alone. I liked to read, to spend time in nature sitting still and watching wildlife. Animals are very open and people put up screens.

Margaret

I was always active, always exploring. I played cowboys and Indians with the neighbors. I had a very active imagination...created places in our yard for building forts and pathways. I imagined the world of King Arthur and the intrigues that took place at court.

Elaine

Comic book reading was my favorite pastime, but I also read books – reading was an important part of my life. I also played board games or imaginary games with my friends. I particularly remember playing cowboys and Indians. I also loved riding bikes into the country to explore. I always had an affinity with nature.

Norris

I grew up playing cowboys and Indians with my friends, climbing trees, and exploring the foothills nearby. I was often accused of having an overactive imagination. I had an imaginary friend for three years who was a very vivid presence in my life.

Peter

One could argue that imagination is another sensory organ, a way of extending the boundaries of one's world. Clearly for the individuals I interviewed it was an active element early in their lives. What is also clear is how the function of imagination continued to evolve in the course of their lives. The development of perceptual acuity or "multiple intelligences," to use Howard Gardner's phrase (6-18), beyond the early interest in playing "make believe" is indicative of this evolution, as Attachment 5 illustrates. While some of these aptitudes proved to have an economic by-product at various times in their lives, the more instrumental goal they serve is to widen the range and deepen the nature of their explorations. To refer to their interests and abilities as evidence of multiple intelligences makes this point more clearly. However, I am not proclaiming a theoretical link between Gardner's research and the aptitudes of the leaders in this study. I am noting that the use of the word understanding as a definition of intelligence is more than an ability to solve problems. It is a capacity for learning that has as its goal new vistas, new worlds, and a wider perspective.

What is it that moves people from one state of being to another? Is it an awakening much like a door opening onto a new world? Is it a remembering of something we always knew and are now amazed we had forgotten? Is it a glimpse of *the fullness of life* just outside our frame of reference? Regardless of how we describe the experience, a change in orientation is the result of an altered picture of reality. For the leaders in this study, a principle objective of their learning agenda has been and continues to be an exploration of the void behind the apparent reality of the universe and the change in perspective that ensues. Their development of multiple intelligences is merely an expression of different ways of conducting that exploration. For self-transforming individuals, reveling in what more there is to learn is more relevant than having a fixed destination. As George Leonard, the author of *Mastery: The Keys to Success and Long-term Fulfillment*, once told me when conducting a workshop at Esalen, "we can practice to achieve our goals or we can have goals to enhance our practice." Requisite to making this distinction is imagination and the will to use it for probing beyond what has already been achieved and what is already known to discover what is yet to be done.

Anticipation of Liminal States

Liminality is a description of the transitional phase between different existential planes. The definition can extend to a number of categories such as ritual practices (rites of passage), time (twilight or changes of seasons), physical location (the edge of a forest or other points of spatial change), and identity (mixed ethnicity or transgender sexuality). Within the ritualistic practices of modern culture a classic example is the state of being engaged. This is a liminal state for those who are neither single nor yet married. It is also a state whose boundaries have a powerful effect on others. I remember the confusion and embarrassment I felt in college when attempting to ask a girl for a date only to learn she was recently engaged (sans ring because her fiancé was in another city and had not yet given it to her). My clumsy reaction, due to feeling I had committed a forbidden act, was really quite amusing to her now that her search for the "right person" was seemingly resolved. The liminal state of engagement can result in a unique perspective on courtship (the past), which may have accounted for her reaction. At the same time, with their goal close at hand but not yet attained, the engaged have time to reflect on the marriage that is yet to occur (the future). Engagement is a period of new awareness resulting from an in-between state and it is this temporal boundedness that gives it a magical quality.

Describing the leaders in this study as well acquainted with liminal states applies not merely to the typical categories listed above but also to states of consciousness. In the use of the hemi-sync process at TMI, exposure to the threshold between waking consciousness and the different focus levels associated with changes in brain wave activity is a liminal state whose frequency of experience is a differentiating aspect of their lives. As mentioned before, the idea of expecting the unexpected when attending a TMI program is learned through the practice of opening one's field of vision to new horizons and then grounding or integrating that experience. Repeated frequently enough, this becomes a way of being; the unbounded state between the past and the future, where something is going to change even though it isn't entirely clear what. How that translates into the more mundane dimensions of their lives can be seen in the way they explore their hopes and fears. Wherever a boundary shows up, whether in terms of vocation, relationships, or personal interests, it merely becomes an invitation for further inquiry, which sometimes means testing the nature of the boundary. As Frank noted about his array of personal pursuits, "I am trying to address my fears." In his case, he has learned to skydive, sail, and ride motorcycles. However, his endeavor isn't limited to physical activities. He also has what he calls "a conservative Christian friend" with whom he has "an ongoing conversation about death and the afterlife." Whatever he might have experienced for himself regarding the nature of death, he is ready to evaluate it in the light of another perspective, especially one that may be opposed to his own.

Anxiety is a natural response to whatever disturbs that which gives us stability, identity, and a sense of belonging (i.e., our comfort zone). Liminality is an appropriate description of those times when we are aware of a moment of choice between what has been and what can yet be, between who we think we are and a blinding insight into what we are. It is a point of demarcation that can be mere seconds in length or a no-man's land where we can wander for years. It is a transitional state where the boundaries of our world no longer seem solid and our past is no longer a predictor of what is going to happen next. It is a troubling time, but not an unusual state of being, as Nietzsche's insight attests:

Those thinkers in whom all stars move in cyclic orbits are not the most profound: whoever looks into himself as into vast space and carries galaxies in himself also know how irregular all galaxies are; they lead into the chaos and labyrinth of existence (175).

The leaders in this study have learned to consciously spend time in the white space, the unformed potential or prima material of our lives. They actually seem to enjoy it as if it is part of a practice in the artistry of their own lives. They use phrases in talking about their lives, such as:

Stepping more fully into life (into possibility) rather than walking around the edges

Gwen

Wanting to trust a journey I do not understand

Helen

Seeking those moments when you can witness the manifestation of spiritual forces

Isaac

Becoming unsettled is important to learning

Kenneth

Watching my inner resistance

Beatrice

Making a conscious decision to live in this world

Regina

Learning what being more awake means

Lyle

From certainty, to uncertainty, to certainty is what defines me [a reference to a continual loop between polarities]
Peter

An experience Carl shared characterizes the liminal state taken to its transcendent conclusion. He was explaining what happened to him one day while he was driving. Suddenly,

> everything just vanished and I am in an eternal moment as a point of consciousness that can see in all directions. There are lines of light going away from me; my possible and probable futures... And between every moment Here, I am in a moment There, and I am holding different memories of the future and the past, every moment. It kind of reminded me of the white space between each frame of a movie picture.

When I asked what is different for him now, he replied, "in a way nothing and in a way everything."

To navigate one's life unconsciously based on assumptions derived from past experience is like having a hammer and seeing every problem as a nail. It is a logical orientation only to the degree that past experience applies to the present or current context. And current context is to a large degree a result of what we are capable of seeing or envisioning as Richard Tarnas noted:

> Although there exists many defining structures in the world and in the mind that resist or compel human thought and activity in various ways, on a fundamental level the world tends to ratify, and open up according to, the character of the vision directed towards it (406).

Such is the function of self-transforming individuals. They are more likely to question their existing assumptions in the light of what more there is to learn (or unlearn). They are more likely to suspend judgment, which as Jung wrote, "is always based on experience, i.e., on what is already known [and] as a rule it is never based on what is new, what is still unknown, and what under certain conditions might considerably enrich [consciousness]" (*CW* 8: 136). In other words, one of the principles I have learned from these leaders is the value of liminal states as a means for building greater capacity for openness to "what is still unknown."

Relationship with Inner Guidance

When referencing transpersonal experiences, which these individuals do in a variety of ways (often without using the term transpersonal), it raises a categorical question requiring a definition. The idea of the transpersonal emerged in the last century and is used by Jung to describe his notion of the "collective or transpersonal unconscious" (*CW* 7: 103). Then during the 1960's a group of psychologists, including Abraham Maslow, the founder of humanistic psychology, developed the concept of transpersonal psychology to "embrace the spiritual dimension of the human psyche" (qtd. in Grof 2). Evident in these uses of the word transpersonal is the idea that the ego-based personality with its organizing function of consciousness is but a part of a totality, conscious and unconscious, that Jung called the Self (*CW* 6: 789-791). Within this totality is a spectrum of psychic phenomena that is not limited to classic notions of physics (time-space continuum) or autonomy (I in relation to my thoughts). Boundary violation on either dimension (physical or mental) is often grounds to speak of a mystical experience. The variety of experiences cast as mystical has been well documented by Michael Murphy, co-founder of the Esalen Institute, in his book *The Future of the Body* (the title alluding to the fact, in Murphy's thesis, that what we call mystical is a form of meta-normal human functioning or human potential yet unrealized within a normal range of functioning).

Robert Forman, founding co-editor of the *Journal of Consciousness Studies*, in his book *Mysticism, Mind, Consciousness*, makes a further distinction regarding mystical experience by distinguishing between "intentional consciousness" and "awareness per se" (112, 131). The former is what we use in crafting our worldviews and, therefore, is indicative of our stage of development. The latter has always existed independent of meaning. Implied by "awareness per se" is a consciousness unbounded by time or space. From where it stems is no place and every place. It has many names and they are all symbols of the ineffable principle of existence - Yahweh, Tao, Godhead, "a being beyond being and a nothingness beyond being" (Meister Eckhart 178).

The following dream I had some years ago is a useful example of the distinction Forman is making:

It is late at night and I am standing outside a large, limestone building of classic Victorian construction. Around me are a number of dwarf-ish, shadowy individuals who are breaking into the building (they are ill defined because I cannot make out their features or the details of their actions, but I know what they are doing). In my arms I am carrying a small child who radiates with a serenity that beguiles its infant state. I exhibit a level of excitement about what is happening that seems to go unnoticed by the child. Somehow I know that the child has had a vision, as the child often does, and I am actively pursuing clues to uncover the nature of this vision. I am seeking artifacts, text, and pictures I can hold before the child to see if a glimmer of recognition appears in its eyes. My diminutive friends are breaking into the building because I believe within are a number of promising clues.

Once inside the building I move rapidly down long corridors extracting one artifact after another from the shelves along the walls to hold before the child. For a period of time the child shows no interest in what I am doing, remaining quietly content and unperturbed. Finally, I notice the child's eyes focus on one particular fragment. As I turn to look at it I begin to awake from my dream and in that instant I recognize it as a tablet from the ancient Mesopotamian text *The Epic of Gilgamesh*.

Putting aside the personal significance of the imagery, the dream illustrates several dimensions of the concept of Self. My dream "I" is an accurate depiction of the interests, motivations, and behaviors of my waking "I" - my sense-making role or intentional consciousness. What "I" am seeking are answers to extraordinary events, visions, and dreams - epiphanies - channeled through a dimension of the Self represented by the child (who is present to my dream "I" but slightly out of phase with my waking consciousness). The dream acknowledges this dimension of the Self by providing it with physical representation, though, interestingly, I cannot tell if the child is male or female. In my dream, the child is without desire, that is, it has no need to make meaning from its existence or experiences. Thus, it is a representative of "awareness per se," what Forman also referred to as a pure consciousness event (6). As the child exists non-physically, one could say it knows "spiritually" all things all at once across existence (it is non-distinct from the object of its knowledge). On the other hand, "I" know by means of contrast and comparison with something already known sequentially over time within the plane of my physical existence (I am distinct from the object of my knowledge).

Forman called the two orientations and their epistemological structures "the dualistic mystical state" (150-151). In his definition, the pure consciousness event represented by the child is no longer a temporary state (a peak experience), but co-exists simultaneously with engagement in the world. It is the phenomenon of intentional knowing, or knowledge by direct sensory contact or through conceptualization, combined with non-intentional knowing, or the pure consciousness event or awareness per se. In other words, the dualistic mystical state knows the self reflectively simultaneously with seeing, acting, thinking. The result is a permanent presence of awareness which can be characterized as an unchanging silence within – the state of openness to what wants to be expressed through us. The way this shows up for most of the individuals in this study is through an ever-present sense of guidance:

> There is a deep peace to me. I don't worry about life being fair. In the great realm of things, it all gets sorted out.
>
> *Peter*

> I felt the emergence of guidance in my life when I began meditating over 40 years ago. I became the ocean that I am.
>
> *Isaac*

I am conscious of a quiet or a peace that is always present behind my ego.

Margaret

The feeling of the higher self being present never leaves.

Carl

I always had a strong presence of guidance [which has been experienced as] a sense of grace most of my life. Rather than struggling with my choices, I have felt guided to go through the open doors the universe has provided me.

Deborah

I am now in a state of silence even in the midst of others. As emotions come up I can witness them.

Kenneth

I have a sense that things lead where they are meant to – the sense that I had to learn certain things before other opportunities emerged.

Lyle

For more than a decade, I have been consciously following the guidance of my "wider self" (I prefer this term to higher self). I use discernment, but there is a clear sense of what is true.

Beatrice

I have experienced a place filled with love that is always there, a place I go back to whenever I want. It is a reassuring feeling I carry.

Frank

The co-existence of an awareness that is clearly transpersonal in nature with the discerning qualities of our unique mental and emotional apparatus has become a permanent fixture in their lives. What may have begun as a goal, glimpses into the transpersonal waves of awareness, results in something transitory and fleeting, like shooting stars that create a sense of awe and then disappear. The peak experience associated with pure consciousness events is a tool for learning and development, not an end in itself. For those whose forays into the transpersonal are temporary in duration it is but the beginning of a deeper transformation. To stop short of that work is the result of what Jorge Ferrer called "spiritual narcissism" which he described as a failure to adequately integrate spiritual openings:

> The structuring of spiritual phenomena as objects experienced by a subject [leads] to a conception of spiritual phenomena as transient experiential episodes that have a clear-cut beginning and end – in contrast, for example, to realizations or insights that, once learned, change the way one sees life and guides one's future actions in the world (38).

One of the distinguishing differences in my conversations with these individuals and other leaders I have worked with is not merely the expansiveness of their worldviews but the degree of self-awareness evident in their level of self-disclosure. To understand this difference it is important to distinguish between horizontal and vertical development. Within a developmental orientation, growth is a process of change resulting in successful adaptation to one's environment (e.g., social, economic, emotional, cognitive, spiritual). Change can be experienced through the assimilation of new information within an existing frame of reference or state of mental functioning. Here change is an extension of an existing orientation through further accumulation of competence, what is meant by horizontal development or technical change. When a more adaptive change is required to accommodate insights or experiences that challenge our ability to make sense of them, self-transcendence becomes the goal. The sense of self we carry in the story we tell about who we are, where we came from, and where we are going must emerge from a state of embeddedness within its existing frame of reference to acquire a new orientation that includes a degree of objectivity about what we are and the nature of reality that has not been incorporated before. This is vertical development or the evolution of our personal narrative.

While observed behavior can provide clues to individuals' state of development, the key is the mental framework under which they are operating. In other words, how they make meaning contributes to the feelings and the actions or reactions that follow. Language is a critical indicator of one's mental framework. For developmental theorists like Kegan, Lahey, and Torbert, language is the medium for organizing experience. Torbert detailed his four parts of speech, which he postulates are essential to action inquiry and personal transformation, as "framing, advocating, illustrating, and inquiring" (27-30). Kegan and Lahey described changes to four languages that underpin an introspective highway to the center of our internal operating system, "from a language of complaint to commitment, from a language of blame to personal responsibility, from a language of 'New Year's Resolutions' to competing commitments, and from a language of assumptions that hold us to assumptions we hold" (*How the Way We Talk* 8). Such is the value that developmental psychologists place on how individuals talk about their lives, particularly when referencing things that are important to them.

The point I am making about my conversations with these leaders is the degree to which their language expressed their openness, frankness, and vulnerability (more affective in nature rather than merely abstract) when describing the important events in their lives. One reason I suspect for this difference is the lasting presence of an inner awareness referred to as guidance. The confidence they give to this inner guidance is quite evident, particularly when telling stories of decisions and actions they took that ran counter to familial, cultural, organizational, or societal norms. When I probed to understand the abiding value of what at times could appear to be a flippant reference to this invisible force in their lives, I was always surprised with what I heard. To give but one example:

What have I learned from my guidance? How to awaken to the truth of who I am by recognizing the shame and guilt I still carry and to love myself as I am. I have carried an unknown wound throughout my life [she was sexually molested as a child]. I saw the effects of it but didn't understand it.

My first insight into healing was taking responsibility for my own feelings. My second insight was to discover that there is nothing in the terrorist that isn't also in me. My third insight, the universe is a mystery. Let go of the idea of ever figuring it out, of putting the pieces of the jigsaw puzzle together once and for all.

Beatrice

There is a paradox of control within their lives that is instrumental to these leaders' state of being. On the one hand, they are actively engaged in the world. As previously noted, their identity as leaders crosses multiple roles including being parents, siblings, sons and daughters, spouses, lovers, bosses, workers, community volunteers, friends, and citizens. They are players in the game of life. On the other hand, there is an undercurrent to them which I became more attuned to in the course of each interview. What emerged was a deeper dimension of self, their own version of a divine child they carry whose choiceless awareness instilled a distinctive energy. Call it the witness state, but their familiarity with it is an obvious source of comfort and one for which they feel gratitude as a means of continuing insight into their own lives and purpose in the world.

Playfulness Towards Life

The more time spent consciously operating across the spectrum of consciousness, the less one tends to identify with perspectives formed by a more limited range of consciousness. The relativity of this statement is obvious, but the intent is to suggest that transpersonal experience begins a journey that alters fundamental premises about one's self. Jill Bolte Taylor has provided an excellent description of her initial struggle to assimilate the experience of being more than her physical body. When a blood clot in the left side of her brain shut down neural pathways affecting her ability to see herself as a distinct personality bounded by a physical body, she had her "stroke of insight:"

When I awoke later that afternoon I was shocked to discover that I was still alive. When I felt my spirit surrender I had said goodbye to my life, and now my mind was suspended between two very opposite planes of reality. Stimulation coming in through my sensory systems felt like pure pain. Light burned my brain like wildfire and sounds were so loud and chaotic that I could not pick a voice out from the background noise and I just wanted to escape. Because I could not identify the position of my body in space, I felt enormous and expansive, like a genie just liberated from her bottle. And my spirit soared free like a great whale gliding through the sea of silent euphoria. I remember thinking there's no way I would ever be able to squeeze the enormousness of myself back inside this tiny little body.

The shock she spoke of isn't merely the amazement of a pure consciousness event – her spirit "gliding through a sea of silent euphoria" – but also, the attempt to reconcile the expansiveness of that transpersonal awareness in terms of physical limitations (i.e., "putting the genie back in the bottle").

The challenge is not unlike what I had to deal with upon returning from my initial program at TMI. While not as dramatic as Taylor's realization she was still alive, I nonetheless felt a disorientation that had long-lasting personal implications. The way I experienced the hemi-sync process was as if the filters of my mind had dilated, resulting in guided excursions beyond my ordinary knowledge (I felt like I was dreaming while awake). Over the course of the program the aperture became so open it literally took several days upon returning home for it resemble anything like what it once was. However, when I had become reasonably grounded, I was surprised by the maze of stimuli I was not able to process very effectively. I became increasingly unsettled by how I now experienced myself and, in succeeding weeks, grew more disconnected from the person others referenced when speaking of me. It led me to seriously wonder about the truth of my own identity. Is my self-awareness a private reality? If so, on what basis is it true? Questions such as these did not ease my transition. The more I attempted to find something to hold onto, the more it merely accentuated the rumblings from deep inside of me.

In time I slowed my thought process – too much effort to process too much information only short-circuited what I was not in control of anyway. I took to sitting and observing without purpose, particularly when I was away from the more familiar contexts such as home and office. A few weeks later, I was sitting idly in the gate area of a major airport awaiting a flight and watching people come and go when suddenly I wondered to myself, "How would I describe myself in a sentence or less?" Almost immediately an answer emerged in my mind, "a stranger in a strange land." Though startled I remained in a meditative mood and began to have a vision of myself wandering among an alien race of people unaware that I was a foreigner among them. This "stranger" was troubled by a sense of fear and resentment, but had no reasonable explanation for the cause of his disturbance. And then the vision faded.

Unknown to me at the time, I was in transition. One life had ended and another was beginning and there were things I was still shedding, mourning, and trying to honor even as I was moving toward a new identity. It wasn't just a change in self-image, it was a change in a way of perceiving – a shift in mental functioning. The notion of being "a stranger in a strange land" was not coincidental or merely a literary allusion. What I didn't want to acknowledge is what the leaders in this study have accepted – we are all aliens. It is an observation they shared not in derision but in a state of musing aloud as if coming out of a reverie. In the course of each interview, there were unprompted stories or insights that I surmise was the deeper dimension of their Self speaking to me. At the same time, there was almost a tongue-in-cheek quality about some of these revelations – a playfulness even as there was seriousness in the message. Listening to the following quotations with an ear for this subtle dimension reveals an attitude about life that can embrace wholeness in whatever form that takes, even if it initially overwhelm one's ability to make sense of it. And when that boundary of understanding is breached and "I get into a state where fear enters," as Margaret noted, "I can let go of the fear:"

> I built up a lucrative practice [as a writer], went on tour and was featured regularly in the media. The part of me that was flying wasn't the part that was meant to fly. A near-death experience in an automobile accident brought me back in the groove again.
>
> *Regina*

It is all about embracing what IS without having to change things. I don't give a rat's ass for metaphysics or theology. I have never been a searcher. I have never been a wanderer. I was just where I was... More divine Mother energy is coming through me now – I am more of a girly girl.

Beatrice

In any reality, it is impossible not to hold our higher self consciously, and yet we are attempting to do it. We are all completely mad, mad as hatters, living a delusion that we are separate from our higher self.

The inner search for the absolute has been the firmest direction of my intention, my interest. And in this reality there are so few absolutes. The only one that I have found is that belief precedes reality.

While I agree that we are that which existed before creation, once creation started, once we separated ourselves from that which is, we became I or god, and with the "I" thought came the "I am," the equal peace with the oneness, and with that original separation from that which we are came creation. Creation is eternal, we can't turn it off. There is only endless experiencing, we can't turn it off. This is my belief.

Carl

I enjoy my life though at times I miss having someone to share intimate things. I am not sure I am willing to do the give and take that is necessary for living a full life with another person...

I have a cottage on 30 acres in Wisconsin which I use as a retreat. This summer I was floating on a raft on the lake and I had an encounter with a male loon who came within six feet of me. I had a strong sense of merging or union with this wild bird. It is now one of my highlights.

Helen

A favorite memory as a child was when my parents would go to Mr. Fan on a regular basis to get "an adjustment." Mr. Fan was a professional wrestler who became a masseuse. He was a huge man, reminded me of a Sumo wrestler. One day he was working with my dad at our home and after observing my brother for a few minutes, asked my dad how long my brother had been deaf in his right ear. My dad had never told him that, but my brother had been born using forceps since my mother had lots of problems in childbirth. The result had been a shifting of the bones behind his right ear that had gone undetected since birth though he could not hear. Mr. Fan asked my dad, "Would you like me to fix that for you?" After getting permission from my father, he took my brother's head and hugged it to his chest. He twisted the bones in his skull and his ear popped open. It has been fine ever since...

Mr. Fan had special skills, I would suspect.

Peter

My first horse was really, really kind. I needed that at the time. My second horse was a tough customer. It was a question of rhythm and lightness with that horse. My third horse came off the Mexican Olympic team, but had been ruined as a result of some terrible vices. It was a question of retraining, becoming light and soft. I learned how to be in perfect balance – to find my balance in balance with the horse...

Breaking my back [when thrown from a horse early in her career] taught me to be more balanced because I couldn't carry weights.

Margaret

Obviously, there is a further subtext to each of these individuals, but the lovely way they were fearless in their disclosures, conveying a sense of wonder, displayed an other worldliness. Integration means acknowledging their change in perspective, even reveling in it. "There is a stamp you acquire. You don't think in conventional terms," is how Isaac described it.

Herman Hesse, a Nobel Prize winning author, wrote a story of a young man, Demian, whose sense of his own difference alienated him from others. Demian was repelled by the brutality of the world and lonely at the same time. Yet, his fear ran deep. He could not accept the "stamp he had acquired," which is the mark of his essential nature. As Hesse noted, every one has but one task, "to discover his own destiny – not an arbitrary one – and live it out wholly and resolutely within himself. Everything else [is] only a would-be existence, an attempt at evasion, a flight back to the ideals of the masses, conformity and fear of one's own inwardness" (111). The implication, for the participants in this study, is openness to the unfolding of their lives and the associated vulnerability that follows. It is a scary proposition to be out on a limb not knowing where your path leads with only your inner guidance to trust in. Many remain fairly solitary figures with relatively few close, intimate friends. A stranger in a strange land they may be, but beyond the courage to accept their "path" and live it wholly and resolutely, there is a lightness to them that plays on life's subtle energy like a butterfly on a summer breeze. They have seen themselves in their essence and know, as Olivia shared, what they are "without all the baggage accumulated in this life."

Compassion for Oneself and Others

In spiritual traditions, it is not unusual to speak of compassion as a sign of enlightenment. William James, one of the early social scientists to investigate and categorize spiritual experience in terms of psychological functioning, reviewed the case files on hundreds of individuals to explore the relationship between mental health and spiritual vitality. In his seminal work delivered as a series of lectures that was later published as a book titled *The Varieties of Religious Experience*, James determined that there are four "qualities of sanctification [that arise with] the attainment of a new level of spiritual vitality:"

1. A feeling of being in a wider life than that of this world's selfish little interests
2. A sense of the friendly continuity of the ideal power [Higher Self, Atman, Tao, God, etc.] with our own life, and a willing self-surrender to its control
3. An immense elation and freedom, as the outlines of the confining selfhood [ego] melt down

4. A shifting of the emotional centre towards loving and harmonious affections, towards 'yes, yes,' and away from 'no,' where the claims of the non-ego are concerned (193-94)

While I wouldn't expect the leaders in this study to describe themselves as enlightened, many of the qualities James identified are evident in their lives. Furthermore, there is a distinctive element to their lives in the notion of a "shifting of the emotional centre towards loving and harmonious affections," what I term compassion, which first had as its objective addressing the trauma of their own lives.

In each interview I explored family background, childhood, friendships, and educational experiences. I continued this line of inquiry into the adult years adding the dimensions of work, intimate relationships, and personal development to the conversation. I asked about pleasant and unpleasant experiences or memories and important events or occurrences. Personal trauma was readily evident in their stories from the time they were born up to the current day - emotional and physical abuse, serious injuries and illnesses (near fatal in many cases and debilitating in others), marital divorce and broken engagements, and the death of loved ones. These are not people who have lived sheltered lives. Their struggles have been heart wrenching, but they tell their stories with an honesty that displays no self-pity or remorse. Without being too graphic, below are two representative examples of the kinds of things they shared with me:

I have had a long-term relationship with the thin veil that separates the Here from the There. Over the course of my life I have spent many years in various hospitals having suffered from Crone's disease and survived four near-death experiences.

Regina

When my first husband reached his mid-twenties he became seriously disturbed and eventually committed suicide after we had been married for 15 years. I would have left him because he was abusive to me and one evening almost killed me. I learned that love can't fix everything.

Margaret

Behind their disclosures is an awareness of the consequences of their trauma in terms of a loss of self-confidence, heightened anxiety, depression, alienation, and splintered egos. The straightforward way in which these leaders spoke of their shortcomings and the inner work they have done and/or have yet to do demonstrates a high degree of personal objectivity. But beyond that, I discovered a level of extraordinary care they feel they have received and continue to receive in their lives. They point to it in many ways from how they address their fears, to how they perceive their lives and their choices, to how they interact with others:

> I now feel I don't need to fit in before using my gifts [as a healer] to help others take their next step. I know I don't heal people. It is their own inner state that leads to their healing.
>
> *Deborah*

> All my life I have felt there was always something other than me that took care of me.
>
> *Frank*

> The irresistible forces in my life seemed to condemn me to bouts of depression that left me struggling for understanding. When I had a heart attack, a light filled my existence with an experience of love that overwhelmed me for days. Since then I have felt a sense of acceptance.
>
> *Isaac*

> I began to forgive myself for some of the things I was still judging myself harshly. Essentially, I have learned to take responsibility for my life rather than getting stuck in the victim role of trying to please others.
>
> *Julie*

> Fear of being molested, of not being able to say no [something that happened at the age of 3]. Over the course of my life, I have intel-

lectually experienced being molested from every angle. I have done a lot of healing to recognize the shame and guilt I still carry, but I am learning to love myself as I am.

Beatrice

I am still the same person, but more in process of maturing in the way I react to life or others. I am not frightened or unnerved by most situations I face.

Kenneth

I have learned to accept the healings wherever and whenever they are offered me.

Lyle

I was in a car crash as a teenager. I was terrified when suddenly I felt these hands on my shoulders and I knew I was safe.

Carl

The healing that has occurred in their lives, resulting in a qualitatively different self-regard, is not a short-term experience. It has been underway for years, as most of them realize. The difference in their understanding is an acknowledgement that, as Margaret described, "I was always protected."

What is the source of this compassion, which has allowed them to overcome so many hardships? What contributes to its conscious presence in the face of their woundedness? The quality of inner guidance has a depth that goes beyond merely a voice speaking to them. Behind that voice or vision or extrasensory awareness is an essence that is more real or true than any conditioned response acquired as a function of the instinctual needs of human existence. It is a lesson made clear to me in the following dream:

I am in the middle of a city and appearances would indicate that this is a seedy neighborhood. Buildings are not well kept and few people are out and about. When I become aware of myself, I am a late middle-aged woman who has been a prostitute. Memories come flooding back to me. I remember the brutality of a life living on the streets turning tricks and the mental, emotional, and physical scars which eventually left me homeless and destitute. I remember how I was eventually hospitalized, but like a bad dream that I awake from now and again I don't recall the details of the institution, just the impersonalized nature of the experience that left me lifeless but functioning.

Now I am living on some kind of state support near the poverty level. I have acquired enough capacity to take care of myself though I still have serious struggles with relapses. But I am aware of what is going on around me. I continue to live close to my old haunts and see some of the old "friends" – people like me who were once young and beautiful. While I am at the hospital for a check-up I pass by a room where I see two women I recognize. They were always inseparable, a twin-billed prostitute act, who went everywhere together. Now they are a couple of schizophrenic bag ladies like I had become. They know something is up because they act like caged animals. Either they have been mugged or merely rounded up by the police and brought in for evaluation. In any case, they are moving around the room mumbling the same things over and over. One is saying that they were only trying to get back to where they belong. The other is trying to get all her belongings back together and ready for inspection.

I can see their world the way they see it. The books they have been carrying look shiny and new and just need a wet cloth to wipe off the dirt on them. But no one will help them. The nurse is complaining that she doesn't know what to do because they are in such an agitated state. I step into the room and look at the books, resisting for just a moment because the empathy I feel for these two women is almost too painful to bear. And then I commit myself and begin to help. I find myself putting the torn cover jackets back on the old, worn books that have been discarded by someone years ago. To my friends, these are precious possessions and none of the hospital staff can see them the way I do, the way my friends do.

As I am doing this work, I hear the buzz around me of the medical staff and I begin to cry. I say out loud to no one in particular, "Why can't people get a little bit of help." As my tears fall upon the book that I am cleaning, I lay my head down. I don't know if I sleep, but it seems that almost instantly the sun breaks through the window in the room and I hear one of the two old women say to me, "Good morning, pumpkin." She doesn't remember any of the events that had moved me to such feelings of anguish. And I sit up and look at her somewhat dazed myself. Then I realize that she isn't in any pain because she isn't present to the world of "today" and I nod and walk out of the room.

When I awoke it was daylight and I was muttering to myself over and over like one of the women in my dream. I felt like crying but I was overwhelmed with the reality of the moment and too amazed to cry. I had experienced my inner state as I had treated it for so many years. And even after the near destruction of this empathic and compassionate force within me, I had yet the strength and courage to reach out to my alienated, fragmented, and suffering self in the knowledge that this sacrifice could be in vain. In attempting to give comfort and succor by helping restore the old books, I risked the possibility that my help would be of little or no value. Nonetheless, some aspect of me was moved to act unselfishly in spite of my own damaged state. This is what touched me so dearly upon awaking, the recognition that in my efforts to meet the demands of my life I had isolated and abused the very source of my humanity, which nonetheless compassionately attended to my waywardness.

As the leaders in this study have learned to acknowledge the extraordinary care operating behind their individual circumstances, they have acquired a similar regard for the suffering of others. It is an orientation based on an understanding they are not the cause of any comfort that others experience, but rather agents in "helping others take their next step." When I heard this expressed by Deborah the image that came to mind was of beings that show up at the time of our physical death. Metaphorically, it applies to the major transitions in our lives when others can appear to help us across the threshold of change and transformation. This work is vocational in the sense of "being called" to be present with others under the aspect of our transpersonal or higher self, what I understand William James to mean in his reference to "spiritual vitality" as the "shifting of the emotional centre towards... 'yes, yes,' and away from 'no,' where the claims of the non-ego are concerned" (194). The following quotations illustrate the point:

> As a result of the energy that flows through me now, the one thing I care about more than anything else is the awakening of whomever I am with. It isn't that I don't have my own desires, but they are subordinate to this guidance.
>
> *Beatrice*

> My purpose is to help show people a space of love that is already there for them.
>
> *Deborah*

> I know I am dying (shedding my skin), but I am hopeful I will have more time here, more opportunity to love. My work is to be a full-time student of life; my exchange is giving and getting love.
>
> *Frank*

> I have a sensitivity, a gentleness, and a concern for others that won't be squashed.
>
> *Gwen*

> My life has been about making changes, and since I have reaped the benefit of these changes, my purpose is to share what I have learned with others.
>
> *Lyle*

> My mantra is pretty simple: Take care of yourself, your family, and whoever is in your charge. I am continually listening for the inspiration about what needs to be said.
>
> *Peter*

Where I am in my journey is to be here now – to be present and of service in helping others realize unfulfilled potential.

Norris

My purpose, which is the covenant I made with myself before I was born, is sharing healing energy to help others through the trauma of the human experience.

Olivia

A touching example of the emotional risk involved in being a "yea-sayer" is a story Elaine shared with me from a longer autobiographical piece she had written. She took up writing in her youth as a way to process what she dared not share in her interactions with others. It was a means of healing to have this inner dialogue. Over the years she wrote many short stories and poems expressing a wide range of emotions in response to the challenges of her life. This excerpted version of her story was prompted by my request to describe her most memorable experience at The Monroe Institute:

Growing up my sister beat me. She was unhappy and ensured that my life was unhappy as well. We had never resolved that. Yet, when she had part of her brain removed I took her on as my responsibility, and had continued to do so for ten years.

She was a child, half of her body was paralyzed, and a chunk of her face had been eaten out by cancer. I recalled an earlier conversation with my partner about what my expectations were for the world, for the Universe and had responded, "I expect a world, a Universe that is generous and compassionate." One day while I sat in my bed at The Monroe Institute, I realized that indeed I had been generous with my sister, but I had not been compassionate. I could barely manage to visit every couple of weeks, did not want to touch her, and could not stand the smell of her. I had had conversations to help her grow when we were younger, but now I wanted to keep my distance.

I called my partner, and the next day after arriving home from TMI we drove the four hours to the nursing home, and I spent time with her. I took Hemi Sync, the "Going Home" CD series, and began that trek with her, using Reiki energy to help protect her when she called out: "A man, a man, an evil man!" and going with her as she smiled in greeting to our mom and dad, whom she could see and I could not. The next few months I tried to visit as often as possible and continued to work through the audio series with her. The weekend before she passed we finished, and she wanted to hear Bob Monroe's words over and over and over again. "Yes" she would whisper from a barely recognizable face above 60 pounds of broken bones stretching distorted skin when Bob said, "You hear and you understand." And when it was time to leave, I pulled her hair back on her forehead, I kissed her, and I told her I loved her. And when she was gone, I grieved. I call it a joyous grieving, for I grieved for someone who I had considered the bane of my life. And I thanked her for helping to make me who I am. Tears come down my cheeks now as I recall and write these events. Every aspect of my life has been surfaced and considered, even my very birth relived, and now much before this life, even to the form and shape that has waited dormant in my "basement."

There is so much unfolding still to occur, so much to learn, so much to experience. Every day I live my life there is some new learning, some new feeling to share with my larger self, some new insight to pass along, some new challenge to grab hold of, and so much love!

The instinctual dimension of human nature exists to protect us and does so in the formation of filters or underlying assumptions which suppress fears associated with pain and suffering. Aspects of self that create a sense of risk (heightened anxiety) are split off and remain unrealized, fragmented, disintegrated. In mythological terms, the journey into the underworld is what the leaders in this study have experienced. And yet it isn't courage that led them out of that wilderness. It is compassion.

The essence of the human condition isn't the programming acquired to protect or shield our woundedness; it is the experience of what Joseph Campbell called "invisible hands" that are guiding us "to discover our own depth." The result is "[we] put ourselves on a track that was always there for us... and doors open where we didn't know they were going to be" (*The Power of Myth* 120). During the years I attended programs at TMI, I raised with myself the question of how to walk in a sacred manner. The response I received from the depths of my soul arrived in a vision of the woman from my previously disclosed dream whose compassion I had abused. Her message was both simple and profound, "First receive my embrace, then embrace others as you have been embraced." Whenever I need an example of what this guidance means, I have but to reference the lives of these leaders.

4

What Difference Does This Make to Anyone Else?

THE ANALYSIS SO far is based on my observation of the leaders who agreed to participate in this study. While I have attempted to be thorough, it is nonetheless my orientation that underscores the way the stories are told. So the logical next question is: How do other people see these individuals? This is where the narration changes as it is no longer my observation of them that matters. What now follows is a more technical description of a common process of leadership assessment using a psychometric instrument. While the process is common, the instrument and the access I was granted to data evaluating two different groups of leaders using this same instrument makes the analysis unique. While I can flatly declare there is no single instrument that can reveal and describe another person, what I can add, based on the analysis, is that I am directionally correct in my assessment that these individuals operate from a post-conventional stage of development. For those who wish to plunge more deeply into the data, the next few pages describe the process of assessment, the instrument, and the analysis. Upon completion of the analysis, I return to a narrative illustration of how I see these leaders at this point in the book.

In attempting to answer the question of how others see these leaders, I chose to use a psychometric instrument that I am familiar with through my own professional practice. The rationale is straightforward. I want the data to be comparable to a larger norm base to reduce my bias in the analysis and I want data relevant to any suppositions regarding stages of adult development. The challenge in gathering data is access. It begins with the personal interest (and trust) of those from whom you want information. I had gained the trust of these leaders for reasons that would not apply to this second set of individuals (call them evaluators) who may or may not care about my purpose in conducting this study and may or may not be comfortable with the degree of self-revelation entailed in an interview (even when the focus of the conversation is on someone else, inevitably there are moments of personal disclosure). Overcoming these barriers would have been a daunting challenge in terms of time, energy, and money, thus, the reason for using an online assessment instrument. Nonetheless, there are both strengths and weaknesses to multi-rater assessment instruments. On the benefit side, they create comparative data relative to a norm base of thousands (if not hundreds of thousands with the larger, better known instruments) and the data are easily analyzed. On the limitation side, they are not contextually sensitive, which means recent personal events of any kind for the evaluators that would affect their perspective are not factored into the assessment (e.g., illness, family problems, promotion, re-location). This is where it is important to have other contextual references for comparison when using any kind of multi-rater instrument, which is what the previous chapters provide.

The choice to use a leadership assessment instrument is merely a function of my familiarity with these instruments. The particular choice to use the Leadership Circle Profile (TLCP) is due to a feature that is not found in other multi-rater assessment instruments that I am aware of. TLCP is based not only on a set of well-researched leadership competencies but also looks at the internal assumptions of individuals as evidenced in their default orientations. TLCP refers to these dimensions of interpersonal effectiveness and internal assumptions as creative competencies and reactive tendencies, respectively. Together, these dimensions closely correlate with Kegan and Lahey's developmental approach to mental functioning in adults. In other words, TLCP captures some degree of insight into how individuals construct meaning from their experiences and what that says about their stage of development.

To briefly summarize, creative competencies measure how an individual achieves results, brings out the best in others, establishes a vision or direction for themselves and others, enhances their own development, acts with integrity and courage, and improves organizational systems (which can include family and community systems). Reactive tendencies are leadership styles that emphasize caution over creating results, self-protection over productive engagement, and aggression over building alignment. These self-limiting styles overemphasize the focus on gaining the approval of others, limiting one's perceived vulnerability, and getting results through high-control tactics. Attachment 6 provides a summary definition of each dimension and the specific competency or style embedded within each.

The 135-item survey is structured to encourage general perceptions of the subject, whether by self or others. While memory of specific incidents is useful, full recall is not required in order to assign a specific score on the 9-point scale (scoring is 1-5 with half points). The following is a sample selection of questions used in the survey:

- He/she forms warm and caring relationships
- He/she creates a positive climate that supports people doing their best
- In a conflict, he/she accurately restate the opinions of others
- He/she learns from mistakes
- He/she exhibit personal behavior consistent with his or her values
- He/she speaks directly even on controversial issues
- He/she attends to the long-term impact of strategic decisions on the community.
- He/she lives and works with a deep sense of purpose
- He/she is an efficient decision maker
- He/she needs to perform flawlessly
- He/she tends to control others
- He/she is sarcastic and/or critical
- He/she lacks passion
- He/she adopts others' points of view so as not to disappoint them

Each of the 18 creative competencies and 11 reactive tendencies assessed in TLCP comprises three to nine items randomly placed in the online survey. The raw score is the average of the respective items for each competency or tendency. The competencies and tendencies are further averaged by dimension, that is, the Relating Dimension comprises the competencies: Caring Connection, Fosters Team Play, Collaborator, Mentoring and Development, and Interpersonal Intelligence; the Self-Awareness Dimension comprises the competencies: Selfless Leader, Balance, Composure, and Personal Learner, and so on through the other six dimensions of the profile Authenticity, Systems Awareness, Achieving, Controlling, Protecting, and Complying.

The results of TLCP are graphically represented in a single circle for quick comparison of self-scores and evaluators. The data are displayed as percentiles (a ranking based on average raw score compared with everyone else in the database). Since the database of TLCP (in 2010) had more than 150,000 evaluators and more than 15,000 self-scores from individuals around the world, the percentile ranking can be quite dramatic in its visual effect. A 15-page report accompanies the graph with summary data on each dimension. Included with the report is a manual that provides detailed information on each competency and tendency to aid in interpretation of the results.

While there are some interesting differences among the 14 leaders who completed the survey (out of the 17 interviewed), it is more important to look at the group as a whole to minimize contextual differences. With a large enough group, individual differences tend to cancel out and while 14 might not comprise a large enough group, it is nonetheless closer to a picture of how these leaders on average "show up in their interactions with others" than any single individual report. Attachment 7 illustrates the composite profile entitled "TMI – The Whole Organization." The black line indicates the average across the self-scores and the shaded gray area indicates the average of the 148 evaluators. The inner circle is a summary of the outer circle by dimension – relating, self-awareness, authenticity, systems awareness, achieving in the upper half of the circle, and complying, protecting, and controlling in the lower half of the circle.

Higher scores in the upper half of the circle demonstrate a higher degree of interpersonal effectiveness in terms of building caring relationships, acting in alignment with one's values, and achieving results. Higher scores in the lower half of the circle may become barriers to interpersonal effectiveness through a tendency to act too cautiously, or with too much aggression, or by removing oneself from accountability altogether.

The collective picture is unusual for several reasons. First, the close alignment between self-scores and evaluators on most every dimension within the inner circle indicates a high degree of personal objectivity. One argument for this is the relatively low complying and controlling scores in the lower half of the circle. Higher percentile scores on the complying dimension tend to lead to an understatement of self (more critical) where on the controlling dimension higher scores tend to lead to an overstatement of self (more inflated). While some degree of understatement is evident, it is not significant. Second, every dimension in the upper half of the circle (Creative Competencies) is in the 75th percentile or higher. As a group, this is quite significant in terms of both the number and the balance across each cluster of competencies. Finding a group of individuals with a common developmental connection such as TMI who collectively demonstrate a superior apprehension of 18 competencies highly correlated with effective leadership is rare.

Finally, the protecting dimension in the lower half of the circle may signal a possible area of weakness for this group. Let's pause here and take a closer look at what may be going on. What this dimension measures (or intends to measure) is the tendency to establish a sense of worth through an orientation of being rational, superior, cynical, aloof, hidden, or distant. The internal assumptions used to organize one's identity within this dimension are based on one or more of the following beliefs:

- For me to be right, others have to be wrong.
- I am worthwhile if I am right and find the weaknesses in others.
- I am valuable because of my superior capability or insight.
- I am safe and acceptable if I remain small, uninvolved, and avoid risk.

Now let's consider the leaders in this study and the context that has been described in the previous chapters. Is this representative of what has been described? In my opinion, yes and no. To say yes means that I can understand them as distant at times (keeping their public and private lives separate), being perceived as having a tendency "to have to be right" and a sense of being "valuable because of a superior capability or insight." However, these are perceptions from the standpoint of the evaluators, who themselves may not have had similar transpersonal experiences and who don't know how to gauge these leaders and their behavioral swings between openness and vulnerability, openness and silence.

On the other hand, to say no means I have also observed their tendencies (1) to step into an observer mode and watch how situations unfold and (2) to take a wider perspective or offer alternative ways of viewing reality. The similarity of these characteristics with the principle of inner guidance, and specifically with a dualistic mystical state, is unmistakable. And yet, what they offer in terms of a wider perspective for those who are not familiar with their own transpersonal self can appear like "adopting a posture of being superior, more intelligent, better, or right." It is a challenge that Joseph Campbell understood in describing the difficulties of integration for those who have stepped through the skin of the world and journeyed in "the all-generating void:"

> The final crisis of the round, to which the whole miraculous excursion has been but a prelude – that, namely, of the paradoxical, supremely difficult threshold-crossing of the hero's return from the mystic realm into the land of the common day... He has yet to re-enter with his boon the long-forgotten atmosphere where men who are fractions imagine themselves to be complete. He has yet to confront society with his ego-shattering, life-redeeming elixir, and take the return blow of reasonable queries, hard resentment and good people at a loss to comprehend... There must always remain, however, from the standpoint of the normal waking consciousness, a certain baffling inconsistency between the wisdom brought forth from the deep, and the prudence usually found to be effective in the light-world...

How render back into the light-world language the speech-defying pronouncements of the dark? How represent on a two-dimensional surface a three-dimensional form, or in a three-dimensional image a multidimensional meaning? How translate into terms of 'yes' and 'no' revelations that shatter into meaninglessness every attempt to define the pairs of opposites? How communicate to people who insist on the exclusive evidence of their senses the message of the all-generating void? (*The Hero with a Thousand Faces* 216-218)

That the leaders in this study have taken up the challenge of trying to bridge between two worlds means facing incomprehension, resentment, and even derision. It is for this reason that the protecting dimension can also signal a degree of spiritual development perplexing to others. In other words, it can signal a stage of development beyond the range or parameters of TLCP to capture.

A further step was taken to evaluate the results of the TMI group profile by comparing them to two other groups that were also surveyed using TLCP. These two groups were selected not only because of TLCP but also due to the use of another psychometric instrument developed explicitly for assessing stages of adult development. This instrument, called the Leadership Maturity Assessment (MAP), is a series of unfinished sentences the respondent is asked to complete about situations across the different roles he or she plays within families, among friends, at work with colleagues or with those in a position of authority where sometimes the needs of different people clash, the context is more multi-dimensional than obvious, and right or wrong is a matter of what perspective is taken. The point of the assessment is to determine how objective the respondents are regarding each situation and what their responses indicate about unconscious operating assumptions or biases. The theory behind this instrument is simply that each stage within the MAP schema has common frames of reference for organizing and expressing individual experience, that is, meaning making, which is consistent with Kegan and Lehay's notion of stages of adult development.

The two research groups were selected to evaluate TLCP in terms of its ability to predict stage development. The first group is a set of participants in the University of Notre Dame's Executive MBA program, a part-time graduate degree program for high potential managers in large organizations (referred to here as ND). Participants are primarily mid-level managers from the mid-western region of the United States who completed TLCP as part of their degree program prior to being invited to participate in the study. Attachment 8 illustrates the ND research group. The second group is a carefully screened set of exceptional leaders who were identified through a network of management consultants and executive coaches working with organizations around the world (referred to here as EL). Attachment 9 illustrates the EL research group.

The objective in comparing the TMI research group with the ND and EL research groups is to gauge or estimate their stage of adult development without having to administer the MAP (one test too many, in my estimation, for a group that had shown a great deal of patience with my many requests). Since all three groups completed TLCP, the results of a multivariate analysis of variance (MANOVA) explains how the TMI group compares to the other two groups with respect to the dimensions most predictive of stages of adult development derived from TLCP. Of the 18 creative competencies, 4 have been identified as most predictive (Anderson):

- Purposeful & Visionary
- Community Concern
- Personal Learner
- Mentoring and Developing

Of the 11 reactive tendencies, 2 have been identified as most predictive in an inverse relationship:

- Ambition
- Conservative

The following table summarizes the results of the MANOVA:

Predictive Dimensions	Group Means			TMI vs. EL			TMI vs. ND		
	TMI	EL	ND	Diff	$p <$	η^2	Diff	$p <$	η^2
Positive Predictors									
Summary of Creative									
Competencies	4.23	4.32	3.97	-.19	.03	.01	.26	.001	.05
Community Concern	4.13	4.26	3.71	-.13	.03	.01	.42	.001	.07
Mentoring & Developing	4.30	4.44	3.88	-.14	.01	.02	.42	.001	.06
Personal Learner	4.31	4.44	3.90	-.13	.01	.02	.41	.001	.09
Purposeful & Visionary	4.34	4.44	3.99	-.10	.07	.01	.35	.001	.05
Negative Predictors									
Summary of Reactive									
Tendencies	2.31	2.15	2.43	.16	.001	.03	-.12	.01	.01
Ambition	2.34	2.34	3.10	.00	n.s.	.00	-.76	.001	.14
Conservative	3.19	3.05	3.52	.14	.05	.01	-.33	.001	.05

Key: Diff = Difference between group means
p = Probability that the difference studied can be explained by chance alone (n.s. = not statistically significant)
η^2 = The size of the effect; proportion of variance in outcome explained by group membership (from 0 to 1.0)

The results demonstrate two clear patterns. First, TMI participants demonstrate consistently lower ratings on the positive predictors and consistently higher ratings on the negative predictors than do the EL participants. Second, TMI participants demonstrate consistently higher ratings on the positive predictors and consistently lower ratings on the negative predictors than do the ND participants. The remainder of this discussion qualifies these differences.

Logic of comparison

Three factors determine the meaningfulness of the differences between group means: (1) the magnitude of the difference, (2) the probability that the difference exists due to chance, and (3) the extent to which group membership drives that difference. Each of these factors is reported in the preceding table as Diff, p, and η^2, respectively. While the magnitude of the differences between means may seem to be the most important, it is equally important to understand the variance underlying those means. The p and η^2 values serve just that purpose. Among statisticians, p values less than 0.001, 0.01, 0.05, and 0.10 are considered highly, moderately, sufficiently, and marginally significant, respectively. In other words, the smaller the p size, the more confidence we have that the results are not simply random. Similarly, but inversely, the larger the η^2 (the effect size), the more the influence of group membership explains the mean difference. The effect size is of equal, if not greater, importance as the level of statistical significance. Since large sample sizes can cause even trivial differences to be statistically significant, the effect size informs us of how substantive differences actually are. Effect sizes over 0.10 and under 0.05 are considered important and trivial, respectively.

TMI vs. EL

The MANOVA results suggest that the TMI and EL groups are similar. While six of the eight means differ significantly in statistical terms, the effect sizes are all very small. Thus, we can conclude that the statistical significance in the differences most likely stem from the large sample size of the EL group. In fact, the largest effect size was just 0.03 for the summary of all reactive dimensions (complying, protecting, and controlling). Given that all these effect sizes are trivial, it would be reasonable to conclude that there are no meaningful differences between the TMI and EL groups along the dimensions compared.

TMI vs. ND

The MANOVA results suggest that the TMI group and the ND group are quite different. All eight dimensions compared between the groups differed significantly. Moreover, group membership explained at least a modest percentage of the variance in all but one of the eight comparisons. Only the difference in *reactive* scores lacked a substantive attribution to group membership. Conversely, group membership explained a substantial proportion (14%) of the variance in *ambition*. Differences in *personal learner* ratings were also noteworthy with group membership explaining 9% of the variance.

Summary

The TMI research group is much more like the EL research group than the ND research group. If these eight factors explain a large portion of the variance in stage of adult development, then it would be safe to assume that the TMI participants in this study would demonstrate comparable scores on the MAP to the EL research group. Based on this comparison, TMI participants in this study are closely correlated with post-conventional adult development. Trying to be any more specific would be stretching credibility of this kind of statistical analysis, and besides, there isn't a need. The point has been made that as a group, the leaders in this study organize their experiences from an orientation that is not inconsistent with my own observations. That I refer to their orientation as self-transforming is less interesting than the illustrations drawn from their interviews. However, the notion that such an orientation or meaning-making ability can be acquired informs the value of the inner work associated with personal development.

Rather than a summary statement of insights and observations, I want to share a story illustrating my experience of the leaders in this study. The story is a recasting of the man who despaired of ever finding his Grail, as told in chapter 2. The difference requires a clarification of the mythic setting of the tale (based on the whimsical story by G. K. Chesterton, *The Napoleon of Notting Hill*). This man was aware of the seriousness of his destiny because he was raised to become a king. The legend of Arthur is not merely an idle boy's fantasy but a part of his heritage. His kingdom has been built upon the successes of prior generations to create a stable world government, so that he will be the last monarch before turning over control to a permanent class of bureaucrats to manage the day-to-day details of a world without nationalistic interests, without meaningful differences, without irresolvable conflict. He has been raised to promote this vision of a new world order by championing the virtues of a government based on the principle of the greatest good for the greatest number of people. It is the ideal of a rational world where the more people share a similar culture, with a similar vision of the future, the greater the number that will be served by the same good. His arguments are impeccable, his logic is sound, and all who hear him are brought under the influence of his conviction to his ideals. He is the most powerful force in the continuing assimilation of individual hopes and dreams into a single vision of progress. But with each successful engagement, each encounter with those few remaining elements that oppose him, he senses himself driving ever faster on a road that takes all of his concentration to navigate without crashing.

The world is becoming gray and drab, losing its sense of wonder, and certainly its sense of humor, as the force of a story he has not written but which he feels compelled to live out overtakes him. The effort takes its toll. He becomes more reclusive, and eventually panic-stricken, as he tries to remain focused while in the midst of a deepening depression. One day he vanishes from the palace without warning. He walks the streets of London incognito, drifting between his thoughts and the events unfolding around him, when he comes upon a boy in Notting Hill who is playing with a wooden sword fighting an invisible foe. In a moment of delight, the king approaches the boy, takes the sword, and proceeds to knight him. He instructs him in the laws of chivalry, as he remembers them from his memories of the stories of King Arthur, and tells the attentive youngster to defend this hill with his life.

By his very actions the king is moved by what once inspired him as a boy in the stories of the knights of the Round Table, the magic of a realm bridging both pagan and Christian worlds, the marvel of knights celebrated for their feats of arms and chastised for their sins, the vision of Camelot – as famous for the tenuousness of its existence as for the honor it achieved. He is touched, as he plunges deeper into his memory, by the poignancy of human courage and frailty, grandeur and humility, passion and love. It seems almost insubstantial as he tries to translate what has captured his imagination in these boyhood memories. How does this apply to who he is as the last monarch of a modern world that has no time or place for romantic foolishness? Yet he is indeed caught in the throes of romance, passion, and an irrational urge to reinstate the pageantry, the gallantry, and the customs of the medieval court of Arthur. He laughs out loud, before turning to make haste back to the palace.

At first, his counselors and members of the transition team refuse even to listen to his idea, but because he has been observed to be in a state of depression, they decide to play along hoping he will soon be restored to a "proper" frame of mind. The king sets about his instructions, requiring all who will appear before him to be dressed in the colors and heraldry of their medieval districts or countries of origin. They are to be announced with fanfare and required to master the courtesies of chivalry. His own counselors will be dressed appropriately in the colors of the court. While all this creates quite a stir, especially for the numerous bureaucrats who have the "business" of the world to attend to, over time a compromise is struck that essentially speeds up the process of transition and places the king in an increasingly honorific role. However, a strange thing begins to occur as the initial years of animosity toward the king for these foolish requirements wane. People are becoming increasingly curious about their own history. The questions they begin to ask of themselves, of those they work with and those in positions of authority demonstrate a sense of pride in their own heritage, their own past. The world was not always as it had become.

The spark, however, that ignites the smoldering heat of rising passions begins as a mysterious, seemingly isolated act of rebellion to the proposed plans to build a super highway structure around the city of London. The plan calls for the demolition of certain older sections of the city to take advantage of the increased traffic and upgrade the economic viability of those areas. This is consistent with the theme of the king's new world order, but which requires, in this case, the destruction of the old merchant district of Notting Hill. A young man has organized a rebellion that is repelling all attempts by construction crews to enter that area. When the king hears of this surprising show of force, unlike any that has occurred in modern times, he calls the leader of this rebellion to appear before him and account for himself. The young man makes his appearance exhibiting the ease and charm of a seasoned court cavalier and then kneels with head bowed before the king. He is courteous and deferential. The king is immediately taken with this young man and compliments him on how well he plays the game, but adds that this is a serious issue and that it is time to drop all charades.

The young man looks up and simply replies, "I don't know what you mean, my lord." The king, astonished, realizes that this is not a game to the young man, but how? Why? Is it possible? The questions begin exploding in his mind. As he presses for answers from this elegant stranger in his midst, he learns of an even stranger story of how this young man has been charged with the duty of defending Notting Hill by the king himself. That moment of inspiration for the king, 12 years before, was a charmed moment indeed, and the vision that he rekindled in his memory was communicated to this young man in a way that even the king did not understand until that moment. But what is the king to do? How can he be true to the march of progress (nobody can turn back the clock) and still be empathetic toward the values, ancient and romantic though they are, of this young man? He is the king, but he is also just a man. He is the leader of the world, but he is also just a small voice in a universe larger than his making.

His is a vision of a world at peace, but a vision that he cannot comfortably live with himself. Regardless of what action he takes, the way things have been will no longer be. As he struggles with himself, he gains his heritage. The questions he has no answers for capture his heart and mind. What the king does in responding to this rebellion, as one might guess, leads to the demise of his kingdom and himself, but it also leads to something he could not have foreseen, a lore that springs up and circulates by way of songs and stories celebrating a new chapter in the dance of life. "The gods were responsible for that, weaving catastrophe into men's lives to make a song for future generations" (Homer, *The Odyssey* 8: 578-9).

The Quixotic spirit that pervades the lives of the TMI research group is not to be judged by those who are ready to settle for comfort, security, stability, and order, in other words, assume a superior apprehension based on what is already known. The view of such individuals is predictably incredulous, even contemptuous of all that is incompatible with what they perceive as good judgment. This is the principle difference I have come to appreciate in these leaders and their personal journeys. In their desire to explore the life within them and the life around them – their inner and outer realities – they challenge the familiar ways of their own lives and what they discover is the "ever-changing center of things, a dynamic quality that is the pre-intellectual cutting edge of reality, the source of all things, completely simple and always new" (Pirsig 133).

5

Thinking and Acting Differently about Change, Leadership, and Organization

Let no day pass without discussing goodness, examining both yourself and others. Life without this sort of examination is not worth living.

Plato (*Apology* 38a)

THE FIRST HALF of this book has been a story of a group of leaders who willingly allowed me access to the details of their lives. Of course their identities have been protected given the level of disclosure revealed in the previous chapters. Nonetheless, anonymity has its limitations. To share specifics around their professional lives within their businesses, departments, or institutions would compromise too much. Yet such a level of specificity is necessary to complete an understanding of how self-transforming leaders affect communities by their pursuit of more life (i.e., bringing something new into being). To remedy the situation I have selected an example of a leader, Dee Hock, who created a portrait of his professional life in his book *Birth of the Charodic Age*. I have judged him similar in nature and approach to the leaders in my research based on the story he has told.

There are two goals to the following chapter. The first goal is to illustrate how transformation has multiple levels (what I call realms of knowledge), which have different degrees of relevance depending on the nature of the change or future state that is being pursued. This goal moves us into the realm of theory and the models I have developed to articulate that theory. As a result, the style of writing now shifts towards conceptualizing what has emerged from the research, as well as my own practice as a leadership coach and teacher, relevant to organization and leadership development. Nevertheless, these concepts will quickly be embedded in examples from Dee's life, and his role as the founder and first CEO of VISA, to illustrate how self-transforming leaders "show up" within a collective context. The second goal, therefore, is to further illustrate that development is not merely self-focused but also collective in nature. In other words, the self-transforming mind is engage in a practice of continually re-organizing experience that incorporates the unexpected as a sought after prize. This is the very nature of being future oriented as leaders in organizations. Tapping the potential of the many accentuates the interaction between the life within us and the life around us in creating what I call emergent thinking which will be further explained in the following pages.

As previously noted, one of the distinctive qualities of self-transforming leaders is the importance they place on an imaginative life. The implications for change and transformation are crucial when noting that Albert Einstein once declared imagination more important than knowledge (1931). If knowledge means a perspective that guides our behaviors, then imagination forms the bridge between that perspective and a new way of seeing the world. Through my work with large industrial firms, I have seen leaders struggle with organization development not because of a lack of knowledge about their business, but because of an unwillingness to address their own self-limiting beliefs. They were not willing to change the way they understood their world and, as a consequence, they were incapable of imagining a different future.

Take for example a major defense firm I worked with as a management consultant. The firm's value proposition changed dramatically when acquired by a large manufacturing company that placed more emphasis on its relevance within traditional business-to-business markets. Here was an engineering-dominated company supported by government contracts that now had to contribute to an integrated portfolio of products for profit-driven customers. The fact that their new customers had business models with razor-thin margins meant that products not only had to be of high quality, but also on time, at or below costs, and serviced from anywhere in the world around the clock. This was a way of life that would alter the identity of the organization, but one that could not be conceived until those leading this business began to understand the limitations of their own worldview. They had become entrenched in a set of management practices that merely extended their identity as a company dominated by engineers. As a senior management team, they enjoyed grappling with technical questions rather than engaging the more troubling concerns of investment strategies and resource allocations. They didn't want to alter the fundamental equity structure of the annual budgeting process because that would require managing the tension between business/financial performance objectives and engineering/product quality objectives. They failed to define a different role for themselves as leaders and, therefore, could not lead an organization that had to transform itself. It is a similar story in many industries.

In the midst of disorientation, organizational renewal is possible, but it depends on the willingness of people, individually and collectively, to look deeply within themselves. The breakthroughs that every organization is trying to achieve in creativity and innovation do not lie "out there" like shells on a beach. They lie inside the individuals who form the mind, heart, and soul of an organization. The true test of leadership in periods of rapid change is the support leaders provide to others to create a bridge between an old way of life and a new future. Not to be found among the myriad details, endless meetings, and late-night deadlines that are choking the life out of most organizations (the more, better, faster with less syndrome) are those clarifying moments when people know what they are a part of and why it matters. In the absence of such moments, a profound loss is felt that can appear as a nostalgic yearning for "the good old days." While a romantic view of the past does exists, in truth, radical change is upon us and not regrettably, as many will profess.

The problem isn't change; the problem is an absence of meaning in the midst of change. The message of our collective development is not change for change's sake and, yet, in the final analysis, too many initiatives in too many organizations appear to have been adopted with just that apparent objective - the implied implication, which isn't lost on people, is it's better to do something, however poorly, than to do nothing. It is no wonder why an array of models and templates for leading change has littered the offices of organizations around the world. Now, in their wake, a new call for meaning has arisen, repeated over and over in interviews I have conducted with executives in global firms over the past 20 years (Baldwin, Danielson and Wiggenhorn, 1997; Baldwin and Danielson, 2000, 2002; Danielson and Wiggenhorn, 2003; Danielson 2010). As one described his company's challenge, "We need to articulate a new story about ourselves" (Baldwin and Danielson, 2002:2). The process of organizational renewal and revitalization is an educational journey and, as such, one that can be guided. However, as of yet, the struggle of leadership is to distinguish the true moments of discovery (learning) from the training venues that have likewise proliferated with all the change programs. The lesson isn't to define the right educational program to lead people through change, like a pied piper, it is rather to understand why people (and, as a consequence, organizations) learn. It is my contention that people don't learn in order to execute the new goals of the organization, they learn in order to find meaning or purpose in their lives.

Individuals, like organizations, are living systems existing between a state of flux (chaos) and stasis (entropy). Stability or meaning is the proper balance between these extremes that sustains the health of the system. Too much change too quickly and individuals lose their orientation. Too much stasis over too long a period of time and individuals lose their energy. Environmental turbulence is a function of the degree of uncertainty it generates and, thus, is addressed through learning or adaptation, which sometimes requires shifts of attitude, emergence of new horizons, or breakthroughs in understanding. Closely linked to the degree of turbulence individuals experience are unique realms of knowledge relevant to their growth and development. Stated differently, knowledge has dimensions that become more or less appropriate for addressing the varying degrees of turbulence posed by the environment or context we experience. The higher the degree of uncertainty, the more fundamental or philosophic are the questions that arise. The lower the degree of uncertainty, the more practical are the questions.

Uncertainty is another way of describing low information completeness and clarity. Mapping these two dimensions depicts a model illustrating different realms of inquiry. In Figure 5.1 the X-axis is information clarity running from high to low. High information clarity describes an environment in which there is a commonly understood goal or vision versus an environment of low information clarity in which direction and purpose are absent. The Y-axis is information completeness also running from high to low. High information completeness describes an environment in which there is significant capability or "know-how" versus an environment of low information completeness in which experience or practice is absent.

Figure 5.1 – Information Completeness and Clarity

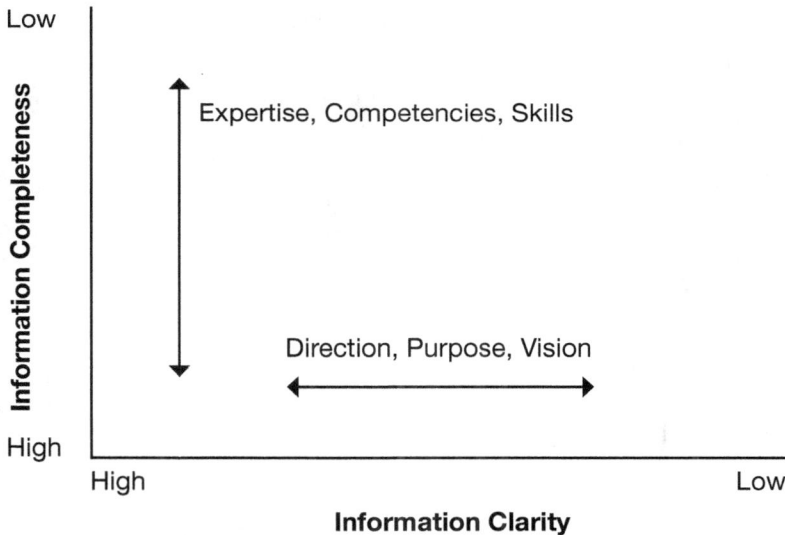

To put a narrative spin on this model is to envision a journey that, on the one hand, leads to the end of an old and familiar way of life (low information clarity) and, on the other hand, illustrates the lack of appropriate skills to function in a new and unknown way of life (low information completeness). Operational effectiveness within any environment depends on the ability of individuals to make sense of the information they receive. Sense-making is many things, but one characteristic of it is the ability to organize data in a manner that can be communicated effectively. Such communication requires a set of filters (symbols, metaphors, models or maps) that screen and organize the seemingly random and incoherent array of data people are bombarded with every day into recognizable patterns. When the speed of change exceeds the limits of an individual's filters to create recognizable patterns, then change becomes unpredictable. Charles Handy called this discontinuous change and a general description of the global environment (9).

As illustrated in Figure 5.2 different realms of knowledge relevant to the function of meaning making exist across the spectrum of information completeness and clarity. With a high degree of both complete and clear information, individuals experience cohesion and integration within organizations. At those times, few have doubts about the direction and strategy of the firm or about the firm's ability to execute its strategy. The collective focus of the organization lies in enhancing operational effectiveness within a given environment. The means to do that is through the applied realm of knowledge where such pragmatic concerns as operating efficiency, product quality, and material costs, for example, are addressed.

Figure 5.2 – Realms of Knowledge

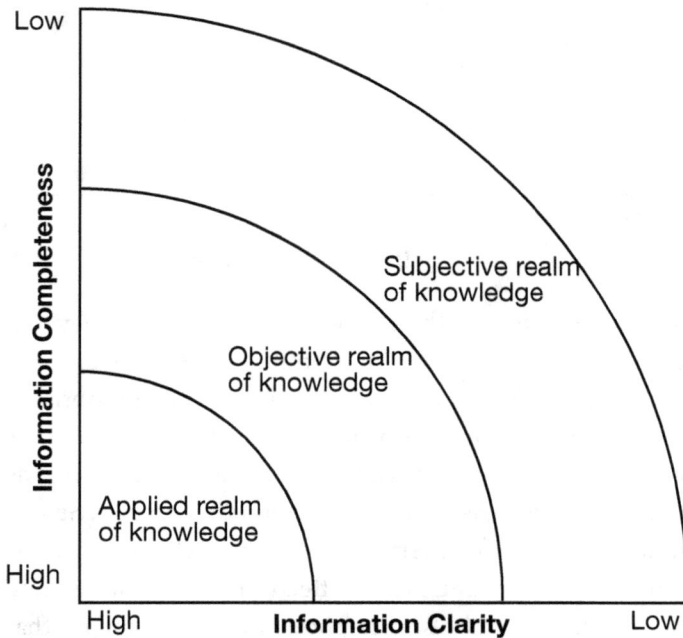

As the degree of information completeness and clarity diminishes, individuals begin to feel a tension between current practices and their overall effectiveness. Questions emerge about the viability of the strategy and direction of the firm. At that point, individuals enter the objective realm of knowledge to adjust the filters (assumptions) used to make sense of the events or data in their environment. Here the concern is with the competitiveness of the firm as measured by its performance in the market. It is a search for insights to adapt the business model (and corresponding strategy that may be explicit or implicit) to a changing external environment.

If completeness and clarity diminish further, the result is a general breakdown in organizational cohesion. What had been taken for granted as a fundamental truth about the business or the purpose of an organization is now called into question. In other words, the boundaries defining a collective identity become ambiguous enough to render the ties that bind people together to reexamination. This is where the subjective realm of knowledge becomes relevant because a shift of perception or consciousness is necessary to alter an understanding of reality. Within this realm there is a suspension of belief or judgment requisite to displacement of underlying operating assumptions. Fear of disorientation, instability, and loss is overridden by the emergence of new horizons that hold more energy than the current reality. What emerges may bring people back together, but more often than not, there is a reformation that drives a collective into more complex organisms within a larger ecological system. The splintering is, in effect, the conscious recognition of a degree of differentiation that had not been sufficiently valued on a collective level.

Each of these three realms of knowledge plays a role in creating, sustaining, and evolving organizational balance, and with it, health and overall well-being. Further illustration will make this clear.

The Subjective Realm of Knowledge

Human beings are highly complex and adaptive systems with extraordinary sensors for gathering data about their environment and incredible processing capability to organize that data. Even so the element that is truly distinctive about the human life system is our reflexive consciousness (Frankfurt 17). We can perceive ourselves. In other words, we possess self-awareness, and while there are examples of other life forms with some degree of self-awareness none has the level of capability that humans do. Like all evolutionary developments, self-awareness creates a system advantage via faster adaptation (learning) leading to even more complex and adaptive capability. Our state of consciousness is the critical differential in the stability of human life and, therefore, expanding or enhancing it will increase our adaptive potential. Toward that end, it is important to note that we are more than our conscious awareness. Consider how we experience our environment. The sights, sounds, smells, and other sensory input that envelop us daily would be overwhelming to process if we didn't have an unconscious means to screen or filter the data. What we perceive of our environment is therefore filtered through a frame of reference helpful to us in addressing the needs of our life (e.g., solve problems, make decisions).

A filtering system is necessary for growth and functionality. However, when this system fails to adequately meet our needs by helping us maintain equilibrium, we experience stress. Our experience is one of not receiving the same degree of clarity and completeness of information from the data we traditionally (often unconsciously) reference. We begin to question why our decisions are not as sufficient in addressing the challenges we face as they have been in the past. At this point we are searching for explanations without fully realizing that we need a way to examine our assumptions in order to become more aware of the guiding principles that have been operational in our lives. In other words, we have begun to lose confidence in the set of filters we have been using to screen the data of our experiences. The challenge of change is extremely personal when the parameters of meaning that frame our understanding of reality become elusive and ambiguous. When that happens, data within our unconscious, or what I refer to as our subjective realm of knowledge, begins to stir restlessly seeking a means of expression. The form it takes is often disruptive to our lives. What we are unaware of we are unprepared for (not predisposed), and consequently, we resist. We struggle against what appears to be an unreasonable force, trying to maintain what amounts to an illusion of control, even as we experience the breakdown of an old way of life.

When a critical set of symbols or metaphors within a society, community, or organization is no longer relevant for individuals, the cultural context is no longer a source of guidance (clear and complete information). Consider the plight of native or indigenous people over the course of the last 120 years. The degree of rapid change to their cultural identity has left many struggling with their personal identity. As the myths, rituals, and symbols of an old way of life fails to communicate a reality that has meaning, that way of life is no longer a source of guidance to the questions of who they are, why they are here, and where they are going (Frazier, 2000). On a very simple level, culture is a collective state of consciousness held together by a shared picture of reality. Consciousness is not an imprecise term, but rather refers to the nature of mental functioning associated with a particular state of existence. For example, a feudal system is characterized by serfdom and the divine right of kings to sit in judgment over the lives of their subjects (even the descriptive nature of the language connotes a particular mentality). Inherent in such a culture is a fate-driven orientation that both dominates perception and gives order to life within that system (Southern 98-110).

In comparison, self-determination or self-interest is a more appropriate description of the guiding assumptions within a capitalistic system. The ability to make individual choices that are perceived as "improving one's lot in life" instills an orientation that life is a function of what you make of it. Similarly, this orientation dominates perception and gives order to individual lives within modern culture. However, no analogy can properly convey the dynamic nature of human life and the fact that, regardless of the cultural context, people eventually inquire about why things are the way they are. Over time, the questions intensify as a result of a widening gap in values between the past and the present. In turn, cultural turbulence increases due to an unresolved tension within the shared picture of reality. If cultures are not to collapse under the weight of their own traditions (which become dysfunctional when they impede development), learning from an *emergent point* of view must occur to cope with the pressures of change.

An emergent point of view, illustrious of a new state of consciousness, arises from the nature of inquiry underway within the subjective realm of knowledge. Inquiry at this level is experiential in form (we experience it before we understand it). This is something often overlooked in the rhetoric accompanying organizational change programs. Merely framing the differences between a future vision and current realities is not enough to actualize change. Absent from that process is the means for *internalizing* change, for creating space for the reconciliation or transcendence of differences. Key to transcendence is an ability to suspend critical attention sufficiently to allow unconscious material to surface. It is what I believe Einstein meant by imagination – to perceive without filters, without judgment. This is not a logical process because there is no way to predict what will emerge. A shift of consciousness occurs when a current perspective that no longer holds relevancy is let go. Without the use of inner or subjective knowledge, there is no means for stepping into the unknown.

An example of how emergent thinking develops is found in the professional life of Dee Hock, founder and CEO emeritus of VISA. Over the first third of Dee's career, he moved through a number of different financial institutions. Common to them all was the resistance he encountered from management to his unorthodox, though highly productive, leadership methods. Not one to mince words, Dee wrote about those early years:

> Conflict between iconoclastic, innovative concepts of organization and management and the iron fists of hierarchical power and orthodoxy [always led to] the same painful result. Just another hunk of unemployed mutton bruised and bleeding on the sidewalk. After sixteen years of unorthodox management and unblemished results, the sheep [a self-deprecating reference to Dee's state of innocence], by the standards of Industrial Age command-and-control organizations, was a complete failure (60).

While Dee had taken advantage of opportunities to demonstrate vision-ary leadership, those very abilities had failed to serve him in his efforts to advance his career within different firms. Why? Again Dee explained:

> During those years the sheep was torn apart by internal conflict. He was filled with desire for acceptance in the world as he found it, for his piece of the American dream. He wanted to believe and belong; to rise to a place among the powerful, rich, and famous. But he was also filled with many things he would not do to get there. Side-by-side with a compelling desire to excel in the world as he found it was an equal desire to behave in accordance with the world as he wished it to be (61).

The conflict between Dee's seemingly irreconcilable desire for career as-cension within the financial world and his desire to change the fundamental operating principles of mainstream institutions led to a cycle of exhilaration and despair that repeated itself like a song he couldn't get out of his head. The words went something like this: Dee would find himself drawn to an opportunity that required foresight, initiative, and innovation. He would immerse himself in the situation, earn the support and trust of his employ-ees, peers, and customers with his ideas and methods of collaboration, and in a relatively short time, enhance the branch office's operating efficiency and performance. It wouldn't take long for the home office to become cog-nizant of his success and quickly reassert itself by requiring adherence to standard operating policies and procedures (under the illusion that if Dee could be this successful on his own, he would be even more successful fol-lowing protocol). The corporate office did not reciprocate the collaborative spirit embraced by each operating unit, and Dee would either be transferred or he would leave the firm under a cloud of frustration and resentment.

With each repetition of this unconscious drama, Dee sank deeper into himself wondering what was to become of him. During those years, he read widely, trying to "satisfy his curiosity about connectedness and rela-tionship" (62). He was searching to understand what he was experiencing and why. But no matter where he looked, the answers were not readily evident. Instead, "out of the maelstrom of experience, study, and stress," three questions emerged vaguely, softly at first, then time after time returning, more demanding and compelling each time:

Why are organizations, everywhere, whether political, commercial, or social, increasingly unable to manage their affairs?

Why are individuals, everywhere, increasingly in conflict with and alienated from the organizations of which they are part?

Why are society and the biosphere increasingly in disarray (62)?

In his ability to give voice to the tension he experienced between seemingly contradictory desires, Dee's horizon on life began to extend beyond the self-limiting beliefs that held him captive. He had found himself stunted by "one's viewpoint, one's frame of reference, one's internal model of reality, in a word, the perspective that experience indelibly implants in each of us" (134). Now willing to look at life through a different set of lenses he "could see with different eyes. Even more, with a different mind. Even beyond that: *with a different consciousness*" (123).

Within the subjective realm of knowledge, an emergent perspective was developing for Dee as a result of reflexive thinking (introspection) and with it a different level of consciousness. The birthing process was long and arduous because it was self-guided. There were few he could turn to and express what he was feeling. Much of what he experienced remained below the surface of conscious awareness and, as a result, he lived through the cycle of an old story several times before he became aware of it. As he began to articulate the inner turbulence that he was feeling, coupled with his directed study of a wide array of perspectives, Dee was catalyzing a change that he could not yet clearly describe to others. He grew confident in his awareness of the change, in his willingness to give voice to it, even as he still lacked a degree of clarity and completeness of understanding necessary to articulate a new frame of reference. Dee was moving ever more consciously into the objective realm of knowledge.

The Objective Realm of Knowledge

An emergent perspective arising out of the subjective realm of knowledge is not a fully developed frame of reference. Meaning is yet dependent upon further elaboration and interpretation to translate a new or stronger inner drive into a source of guidance that reflects reality according to some standard of functionality. In short, the emergent perspective can't yet help us solve problems. When meaning or purpose is found within the boundaries of an existing picture of reality (the objective realm of knowledge), problem solving has a culturally accepted logic to it. This is true whether the problem is exotic (developing the next generation of robotics) or commonplace (choosing a career or livelihood).

Thomas Kuhn referenced the boundary between subjective and objective knowledge when he spoke of scientific revolutions as a change of worldview. He described it as "a relatively sudden and unstructured event," a "gestalt switch" where "scientists often speak of the 'scales falling from the eyes' or of the 'lightning flash' that 'inundates' a previously obscure puzzle, enabling its components to be seen in a new way that for the first time permits its solution" (122). When scientific revolutions occur, "it is rather as if the professional community had been suddenly transported to another planet where familiar objects are seen in a different light and are joined by unfamiliar ones as well" (111).

What Kuhn points out is the relativity of meaning: To the degree that meaning depends on a set of recognizable patterns (e.g., models or maps), it follows that the quality or richness of these models will be instrumental to meaning or sense-making. When new information is perceived because the filters have changed (due to a new worldview), the models or maps of reality likewise reflect a new lay of the land. Thus, the role of critical inquiry is to create a frame of reference that can, first, translate an emergent point of view into a new perspective that provides direction and purpose for an individual and, second, leads to appropriation of that perspective within a larger cultural context. [Note: The reference to Kuhn is not intended to equate science with objective knowledge. The intellectual foundation of any culture is formed on the basis of an ontological premise about the nature of knowledge. To say that individual and collective understanding of truth is reflected in "objective knowledge" means, in my rendering of the phrase, the realm where we organize the data of our experience into patterns or maps that allow us to interact with others and our environment in a meaningful way. Though there are exemplars and injunctions for organizing data, map-making is not an exact science. While critical inquiry is helpful to improving the quality of objective knowledge, the result is not necessarily compatible with a process commonly understood as the scientific method.]

Let's return to the story of Dee Hock and see how a unique combination of events led Dee to clarify and elaborate upon a point of view that would ultimately lead to his role as architect of VISA. In the mid-1960s, credit cards were beginning to emerge across the U.S. with bankcards as the most obvious example. A bankcard was a line of unsecured credit extended to individuals for use wherever that card was accepted.

A fundamental limitation to any bankcard, however, was the merchant system that accepted them. On one side of the issue were the banks. A bankcard would be limited to a relatively small geographic region unless it was associated with a large enough bank to achieve name recognition in many different places around the country (and ultimately the world). On the other side of the issue were the merchants. Having a large proliferation of bankcards would tax the merchant system in processing all the different transactions. To solve this problem, Dee was thrust into a leadership role within his own bank as part of an opportunity to create a "franchise" under the Bank of America name that later became a need to orchestrate a national system of licensees into a single operating system.

Dee recognized the nature of the problem as ultimately a question of perception and, therefore, an opportunity to create a different kind of organization. By redefining the business of credit cards from issuing a line of credit to an exchange of value, Dee and his team transformed themselves from a credit business, with lots of competitors, to an exchange card with no competitors. As he wrote about the challenge:

With compelling need for a new organization, a precarious toehold from which to make the attempt, and the liberty to try, I suppressed my perspective of what the future might be and tried to create the conditions by which new concepts could emerge... After sharing my belief about the opportunity that might be hidden in the problems of the system [with the team I had assembled to help me with this challenge], I asked if they would be willing to take a week or more of their time, isolate themselves completely, set aside all thought of the problems of the system, and address a single question based upon a single assumption: If anything imaginable was possible, if there were no constraints whatever, what would be the nature of an ideal organization to create the world's premier system for the exchange of value (131-2).

Dee noted himself, "my learning would have to evolve in concert with the others" (131).

The struggle became one of giving voice to the "new or stronger life urge" that had begun to germinate within Dee. It was a voice that instructed him, troubled him, tormented him, and tantalized him. It kept him up at night as he wrestled with new concepts and ideas. Learning a new way of seeing or perceiving things, even with the guidance of all that he had already learned, was not what he thought it would be. It was a struggle for definition of his very identity:

When it becomes necessary to develop a new perception of things, a new internal model of reality, the problem is never to get new ideas in, the problem is to get the old ideas out... Clear any room in your mind of old perspectives, and new perceptions will rush in. Yet there is nothing we fear more. We are our ideas, concepts, and perceptions. Giving up any part of our internal model of reality is worse than losing a finger or an eye. Part of us no longer exists. However, unlike most organs of the physical body, our internal model of reality can be regenerated but never as it was. And it's a frightening, painful process (135).

As he began to let go of the old ideas that had dominated his life and his way of perceiving reality, Dee eventually came face to face with the following questions:

> What if we quit arguing about the structure of a new institution and tried to think of it as having some sort of genetic code? How does genetic code in individual cells create recognizable patterns – platypus and people – palm tree and pine – minnow and mouse – yet never duplicate a single creature, leaf, blade of grass, or even snowflake? How does nature create infinite diversity within infinite patterns of infinite complexity (136)?

The result of these questions for Dee was to find the "genetic code" of organizations, which in turn led him to investigate the nature of organizational purpose and guiding principles. As he was to conclude, principles do not prescribe specific behaviors; however, they can induce an infinite array of responses. For example, the principle to "honor thy father and mother" does not describe the form honor would take in any particular situation, and therefore, it induces a variety of behaviors expressing this principle. Similarly, within organizations, principles created through a shared sense of purpose induce rather than compel behaviors.

This was strikingly obvious and simple to Dee (a "gestalt switch"). No set of "leaders" could ever define the means to achieve the extraordinary, to go beyond the limits of the past and accomplish what had never been done before. Only people who govern themselves are capable of such inspiration. And in that realization, Dee gave voice to a new map or theory of reality:

> There is no way to give people purpose and principles, nor can there be self-governance without them. The only possibility is to evoke the gift of self-governance from the people to themselves. It is in that process that a true leader may be useful (90).

As a result of a shared purpose and a set of guiding principles or concepts dealing with the locus and exercise of power, the distribution of rewards, and the voting rights of members, VISA was launched. A new concept of organization had taken root in which ownership is in the form of perpetual, nontransferable rights of participation. VISA is a member-owned organization, but how does it work? How does it enact the principles that framed its charter? What is the practice that grounds the theory?

Map-making is never an exact science, as I have already noted, and yet it must hold up to scrutiny. Critical inquiry is requisite to testing and evaluating an emergent point of view in order to appropriate a new perspective into mainstream culture. Without a shared map of reality there can be no values to guide actions and, consequently, no "problem-solving" efficacy. This was certainly true for Dee as the CEO of VISA and for the other "stakeholders" in this novel venture. However, the test of successful cultural change is ultimately building new capability. Therefore, on the boundary between objective and applied knowledge is a further translation of theory into practice.

The Applied Realm of Knowledge

Objective knowledge organizes the data of experience. The result is a frame of reference or model of reality that can be used to solve problems and address the challenges of daily existence. How a particular model is translated into a set of actions or "solutions" is the function of applied knowledge. Translation is not a literal process. The challenge is converting an abstraction into something imminently practical that remains true to its essence. I have witnessed this challenge on numerous occasions in different organizations. Top management "communicates" a series of initiatives for the business that, for example, entails operational excellence, leveraging new technologies, integration of acquisitions, or becoming more customer-centric, but leaves employees wondering what it means for them. How will their lives be different as a result? What changes will they have to make in what they do? Will they even have a role to play in this new organization?

The disconnect lies in what I call the "new person" or "beginner" challenge that organization development requires. For example, when individuals move into a new organization or professional community they naturally inquire about "how things are done here." There are practices, protocols, and social norms to be learned to demonstrate competency and achieve social/professional acceptance. Even when acceptance is not a primary objective, this level of inquiry is nonetheless relevant to contextual or cultural understanding. As a noted French sociologist wrote:

> Let us add that in this compartmentalized world, there are 'rules of the game,' as in any organization, that is to say a set of codes of proper behaviour, unwritten of course, which each person must respect in order to survive, or more concretely, to avoid being rejected by the other actors. In a more sophisticated form, this is what we would call 'culture'; the set of formal and informal rules which evolve over time, encoding the rights and duties of each person vis-à-vis all others (Dupuy 110).

Within every functioning culture there exists a high degree of information completeness and clarity that has been internalized as codes of behavior and evidenced by the relative prestige granted to those who know what to do under different circumstances (i.e., those who know reality concretely within the context of their culture). To change "the way things are done" is to challenge the status earned by those who have been successful in adapting to their context. Naturally, they want to interpret the message of organization development in terms that will protect their status and therefore they personalize the message according to what eliminates or minimizes risk for them.

Take for example the following story about the re-design of the VISA card itself, which serves to illustrate the knowledge Dee's management team had of "the rules of engagement" with the board of directors. The story begins with the risky, but successful efforts to develop the brand name VISA. In each country, the card had an identity under a different name, BankAmericard in the U.S., Chargex in Canada, Barclaycard in the United Kingdom, Sumitomo card in Japan, and so on. Once VISA became the worldwide brand and acceptance among consumers and merchants rapidly followed without loss of revenue or projected growth, it was assumed within the member organizations that continued change or innovation was no longer critical. However, as Dee noted, "the global name change to VISA" was only the beginning:

> In time, we reached a point where management thought it possible to reduce the size of the VISA name and logo from the face of the entire card to a much smaller logo in the center of the card, opening up space for greater bank identification and co-branding with non-member bank customers. It was the same old story. The customary had become sacred. Reasons why it should not be done came fast and furious. "Bank identification will dwarf and degrade the name and marks" – "Merchant clerks won't recognize the reduced logo" – "Consumers will see the product as inferior and turn to competitive cards with more powerful identification" – "It's foolish to diminish a dominant brand" (265).

The call went out from directors of many of the card-issuing banks for a thorough market research project before embarking on any further changes in the design of the VISA card. While Dee and his management team agreed, they were skeptical about the "efficacy of reliance on statistical, supposedly objective research, for it seemed to result in catastrophic mistakes as often as success" (265).

The mode of inquiry and innovation that had developed among the VISA management team again took center stage. Rather than looking externally for "experts" to tell them how to do things, the management team approached the problem playfully, with freewheeling discussions where nothing was off limits or too unusual to be heard. As Dee wrote:

> We returned to our old habit of peeling a complex mental onion with constant questions. What is the ultimate test of the acceptability of a card? What is the most difficult, most risky card to present and have accepted? Who does it? How is it done? An idea emerged that was compelling. The most difficult card to create, market, and have ac-

cepted was a counterfeit card... What if we were to design a card with a reduced logo identical to what we were proposing, emboss our own cards, and simply present them in the normal way, at normal times, without comment, recording transaction-by-transaction what we experienced and what the merchant said and did (266).

While the plan to "market test" a new version of the VISA card was novel, it had a major flaw. The members of the VISA management team would be suspect in their evaluation of merchant comments when presenting their "counterfeit cards." Therefore it was decided to enlist the support of employees of the outside accounting and law firms used by VISA "asking them to allow us to counterfeit their cards as well and to help design an impeccable process to tabulate and verify the results" (266).

The beauty of the process was that not a single procedure needed to change, no customer would be disturbed, no questionnaire would be created, and no experts had to be hired. All that was required was a notebook in which everyone participating in the "test" would record exactly what happened when they presented their counterfeit card to merchants. The results were amazing. Not a single card was rejected because of the new design. In fact, many responses indicated that merchant employees merely wondered when they would get their new VISA card. "It was as though the public had come to expect innovation from VISA. They assumed that the new model was somehow superior to the old" (267). In short order, the board of directors of VISA approved the changes in VISA card design.

Once again, in periods of rapid change where past practices are no longer good indicators of future success, everyone is essentially starting over. For these reasons alone, it is no surprise that organizations are now going through significant turnover of personnel. When attempting wide-scale organizational change, the difficulty of overcoming the biases and prejudices of people who "have a history" with the organization is often considered a greater hurdle than merely introducing a new set of players. However, this avoids the real problem of cultural change because all people have a history, new players included. Outsiders aren't necessarily less resistant to change, they are just perceived as representing a new way of doing things, which means doing things the way someone else wants things done. Insider or outsider, one orientation is just as likely as the next to impede any fundamental and systemic revision in the way things are accomplished.

Dee Hock acknowledged that the greatest mistake he made was to completely underestimate the degree of individual change that was required to support the concepts upon which VISA was founded. Regardless of how willing people were to be engaged by the openness, the freedom, and the trust within the organization, many felt these characteristics applied "to them in relation to those to whom they reported, but not in relation to those over whom they reported" (276). Due to the fact VISA was so new, success was so immediate, and growth was extremely rapid, a significant number of management hires came into the organization without understanding the growth that was required of them as leaders to support the principles of the organization. Instead they each came into the organization "full of the techniques, culture, and habits of the world from which they emerged" (276). The consequence was more insidious than Dee realized, "I did not anticipate how pervasively and persistently old concepts would reassert themselves, or the covert, tenacious resistance new methods would evoke" (276).

Only by continual innovation in adapting and evolving the concept of VISA was it possible for Dee to reassert the underlying principles of the organization and the practices of self-governance. Evolutionary development or adaptation is a characteristic of any living system. The key is feedback or continual evaluation of performance. Feedback is much easier for an individual or an organization to pursue if self-initiated. That was the beauty of Dee's vision, a set of guiding principles which require continual modification of current business and organizational practices to create unique solutions to unique situations.

While VISA struggled at various times to enact the principles upon which it was founded, it eventually overcame one obstacle after another through the perseverance and inspiration of people who "owned" the outcome (their artistic rendering of the meaning of their shared purpose and guiding principles). By the end of the 20th century, VISA was a member-owned organization comprising 22,000 banks, which competed with each other for 750 million customers and cooperated by honoring one another's $1.25 trillion in transactions annually across borders and currencies. It had grown a minimum of 20% compounded annually (some years as high as 50%) for three decades to become the single largest block of consumer purchasing power in the global economy. It processed more electronic financial transactions in a week than the U.S. Federal Reserve system did in a year and, yet, during that time, it could not be bought, raided, traded, or sold (189). It goes without saying that no set of rules has ever been defined that can apply to every situation or every problem encountered by people each day. Innovation is critical to the success and survival of organizations and professional communities, as well as the individuals who comprise them. As important as it is to know "the rules of the game," longevity is only assured by using that knowledge to create a new story that envisions a different endgame. To address the real problem of change is to both understand and deal with the pain, confusion, anxiety, even fear, that lurks near the surface of organizational life today, for therein lies the means for creating a different perspective to capitalize on change.

Einstein challenged many of the prevailing views on the origin and nature of the universe. In an almost reflexive comment, he noted that "a new type of thinking is essential if mankind is to survive and move toward higher levels" (13). Achieving a different perspective, and increasing awareness of what is yet possible, requires a shift in our "center of gravity" or developmental level. The subjective realm of knowledge is the source of emergent thinking that offers the means for redefinition in the midst of environmental turbulence and uncertainty. In an era of increasing complexity, the challenge is not to create new management practices, though these will certainly result with a shift of perspective, or to create new business processes, though these will certainly follow key insights. The challenge is even more basic, which is to create the means for a transcendent function to exist within the communities of practice that define organizational life. While this is at the heart of a personal practice in the lives of the leaders in my study, the way they "hold space" for others to experience the depth of their own being is what is modeled as a collective practice in the next chapter.

6

Leadership as Soul Work

Every individual, group, society, nation, culture, and civilization
is perpetually in a state of flux and transformation.

Ashok Bedi (105)

T HE STORY WAS told by a colleague who was in attendance at a conference when Mother Teresa gave a keynote address. It was a conference for human resource leaders across India with several hundred present for her presentation. She was introduced to great expectations before she walked to the podium. When she began to speak, she wondered aloud why she had been invited to give a talk to such an esteemed group of leaders. She acknowledged her lack of business knowledge and instead put two questions to the group: "Do you know your people? And do you love them?" At that point, she stopped a moment, looking at the audience before walking off the stage. The silence that followed was deafening and then one individual, a second, and finally everyone began to stand and applaud. Her questions are not typically asked of business leaders. In some quarters, they would be considered improper. However, they are the relevant questions in learning how to listen deeply to the interior life within our organizations and communities.

In his book, *The Reasons of Love*, philosopher Harry Frankfurt links the things humans care about most deeply with the quality of love. One of the criteria of this love, as distinct from charity, is the personal nature of what is loved. There is no reason for it beyond the knowing of the other in itself (a merging of self and beloved). This knowing is experienced prior to any understanding or interpretation of what it means, and even further, from any application in the form of rules of engagement with others. It is without explanation, a mystery from which the motivation and actions of the lover follow. To be one with the beloved is to be "wholehearted" and is the goal even of self-love (95). For Frankfurt, without self-love no other love is possible, a position he felt even Christ noted in proclaiming that loving others is based on how we love ourselves – "diliges proximum tuum, sicut teipsum" (Matthew 22:39). The Latin version of the English translation "to love your neighbor as yourself" makes an important distinction about the nature of this love. The verb diligere means to choose out, prize, esteem, love. It implies worth, and the injunction of Christ is to see and acknowledge that worth in others as we see and acknowledge it in ourselves. But the question yet exists: Do we know our own worth? Are we whole-hearted?

To create the space or environment to embrace, individually and collectively, the challenges we face as a means to grow, we must live a life of fulfillment and build a legacy of value that begins with knowing the difference between perfection and wholeness. In her clinical work as a physician and development psychologist, Karen Horney discovered what she described as the inner pride system that evolves out of the early drama of childhood:

> Under inner stress, however, a person may become alienated from his real self. He will then shift the major part of his energies to the task of molding himself, by a rigid system of inner dictates, into a being of absolute perfection. For nothing short of godlike perfection can fulfill his idealized image of himself and satisfy his pride in the exalted attributes which (so he feels) he has, could have, or should have (13).

Much of the confusion regarding self-love can be understood from Horney's work, which illustrates the narcissistic orientations resulting from self-alienation. When cut off from the "real self" self-idealization replaces self-realization as the inner drive. At first blush, the goal of perfection appears to be a formula for high achievement, until at some point it becomes a tyrannical life leaving the psyche (originally meaning the soul) bound by a "system of inner dictates." Nothing seems to be good enough, no effort, no recognition, no rewards, because it only raises expectations further and, with that, the need for control. To compensate, it is a short step to either begin criticizing others for not being smart enough or good enough, or taking over from them when they don't do things the "right way," or becoming passive and compliant to the will of those you can't control only to complain about them. It is a story not unlike the early career of many leaders in my research, where the reaction of senior management to these young leaders left them often wondering aloud if they would ever be successful. Whatever they did was not good enough or the right way, but behind this reaction was also a reflection of their own self-image in the way they interpreted the instruction they received. They needed to prove themselves and proof of their value was whether senior managers left them alone, not how they were integrated into a larger enterprise.

In my own version of this story, I was quite pretentious in believing I would have a life similar to my romantic notion of famous people. Later when choices had to be made, I heard the doors of my own potential closing behind me and felt a sense of entrapment. As I looked out on the world from my vantage point at the time, there seemed little connection between vocation and personal fulfillment. While I placed a premium on psychic income, I took no particular pleasure in the skills necessary to pursue the life of the mind - code words for a university teaching post. A scholar's life quickly lost its luster amid the long hours of library research. I wanted to be engaged with interesting questions, but instead I found I had to prove myself with uninteresting ones. As one advisor informed me, "It will require 20 years of textual analysis before you can legitimately generalize." Thus began my journeyman years in search of a vocation, and while I vowed to live a life of learning, I didn't understand what the really interesting questions would cost.

Paradoxically, the very inquisitive attitude that initially placed me on my journey ultimately became a barrier to my own development. The powers of investigation I developed to scour my known world in search of purpose and meaning were incomplete. While I had an ability to hold opposing ideas in my mind without immediately rejecting one, my grasp of different worldviews was not nearly as encompassing as I led myself to believe. I grew intoxicated with the glimpse of understanding, the peak experience of insight. To see too much would require change, but to see just enough to tantalize and I could wallow in the pleasure of potential forever. However, not far below the surface of my daily life, a dark foreboding dwelled. There was a shallowness to my life I masked with a focus on personal achievement. While I earned the accolades of others I developed little strength of character. The more I attempted to rationalize my anxieties regarding my direction in life, the more I widened rather than bridged the division in myself. Needless to say, I didn't know how to help myself and with each succeeding action I took there was a greater reaction that belied my sense of control. Finally, my life came crashing down like a house of cards as I sacrificed much that was dear to me in an attempt to hide from my fears.

I lacked sufficient interiority. Ken Wilbur, an American writer and philosopher, summarized the paradox of growth in the following formula: increasing development = increasing interiorization = increasing autonomy = decreasing narcissism. "The more one can *go within*, or the more one can introspect and reflect on one's self, then the more detached from that self one can become, the more one can rise above that self's limited perspective, and so the less narcissistic or less egocentric one becomes" (256). An egocentric view of autonomy is a dark omnipotence that believes "[it] can dispose and bid what shall be right" (Milton I: 246-7). Like John Milton's depiction of Lucifer in his epic poem *Paradise Lost*, I preferred my limited notion of kingship. Though I achieved degrees of control within my own life, what I learned through the dark night of my soul was that I was deceived in believing that control is what matters; it only matters if you are living to avoid your fears and the demons they have created. "Self-knowledge, then," wrote Horney,

> is not an aim in itself, but a means of liberating the forces of spontaneous growth... To the extent that we take our growth seriously, it

will be because of our own desire to do so. And as we lose the neurotic obsession with self, as we become free to grow ourselves, we also free ourselves to love and to feel concern for other people (15-16).

The forces of spontaneous growth are what James Hillman, the founder of archetypal psychology, described as the soul's code. They comprise the DNA of a personality or "the imaginative possibility in our natures" (xvi). Inherent in such a notion is the development journey of self-realization. Choices are not arbitrary but based on what it means to be aligned with one's real Self (with a capital S), the paradox of which is a tension that defies final resolution. The Self is a totality that possesses empirical and non-empirical dimensions. To emphasize one dimension of this totality at the expense of the other is to color life with radically one-sided realities from the magical vision of innocence (i.e., the wonder of mysterious forces behind physical reality) to the deterministic vision of independence (i.e., pursuit of knowledge as a means to control and rule). However, a third position is to see the interdependence of the two as the catalyst of development that activates the soul's code and continually works to bring forth and integrate our imaginative possibilities.

In his clinical studies, Jung observed how his patients overcame dysfunctional patterns of behavior and self-defeating routines when they "brought something new into being," that is, a new perspective:

> All the greatest and most important problems in life are fundamentally insoluble... They can never be solved, but only outgrown... This "outgrowing," as I formerly called it, proved on further investigation to be a new level of consciousness. Some higher or wider interest appeared on the patient's horizon, and through this broadening on his or her outlook the insoluble problem lost its urgency. It was not solved logically in its own terms but faded out when confronted with a new and stronger life urge (CW 13: 18).

By "higher or wider interest," Jung is referring to the resolution of a tension that builds within a state of consciousness when a current perspective no longer holds relevance. Jung called this the *transcendent function*, a technical term referring to the "collaboration of conscious and unconscious data" (*CW 8: 167*). In addressing the tension created by self-limiting behaviors, data that exists below or outside a conscious level of awareness (emotionally charged content) is brought to bear on data that informs a current perspective (mentally constructed models). This notion of "conjoined opposites" in which admitting the validity of the "other" - the physical to the metaphysical, the light to the dark, the creative to the destructive, the conscious to the unconscious, the known to the unknown and vice versa – "generates a tension charged with energy and creates a living, third thing--not a logical still birth in accordance with the principle tertium non datur but a movement out of suspension between opposites, a living birth that leads to a new level of being..." (*CW 8: 189*). The tension at the heart of self-division therefore becomes the means of movement toward wholeness, if we are willing to dive into that tension rather than avoid it. From a mythic perspective, it is not by chance that this is the path we must walk.

In a letter to his brother in 1819, the English poet John Keats called the world "the vale of soul-making." Rather than construing earthly existence as the valley of tears where suffering exists for no apparent reason other than to yearn for death and heaven's reward, Keats proposed a different orientation:

> The common cognomen of this world among the misguided and superstitious is 'a vale of tears' from which we are to be redeemed by a certain arbitrary interposition of God and taken to Heaven. What a little circumscribed straightened notion! Call the world if you please "The vale of Soul-making". Then you will find out the use of the world (I am speaking now in the highest terms for human nature admitting it to be immortal which I will here take for granted for the purpose of showing a thought which has struck me concerning it).

> I say 'Soul making' where Soul is distinguished from an Intelligence. There may be intelligences or sparks of the divinity in millions, but

they are not Souls till they acquire identities, till each one is personally itself. Intelligences are atoms of perception - they know and they see and they are pure, in short they are God. How then are Souls to be made? How then are these sparks which are God to have identity given them - so as ever to possess a bliss peculiar to each one's individual existence? How, but by the medium of a world like this?... This is effected by three grand materials acting the one upon the other for a series of years. These three Materials are the Intelligence, the human heart (as distinguished from intelligence or Mind), and the World or Elemental space suited for the proper action of Mind and Heart on each other for the purpose of forming the Soul or Intelligence destined to possess the sense of Identity...

That you may judge the more clearly I will put it in the most homely form possible. I will call the world a School instituted for the purpose of teaching little children to read. I will call the human heart the horn Book used in that School, and I will call the Child able to read, the Soul made from that School and its hornbook. **Do you not see how necessary a World of Pains and troubles is to school an Intelligence and make it a Soul?** A Place where the heart must feel and suffer in a thousand diverse ways! Not merely is the Heart a Hornbook, it is the Mind's Bible, it is the Mind's experience, it is the teat from which the Mind or intelligence sucks its identity. As various as the Lives of Men are, so various become their Souls, and thus does God make individual beings, Souls, of the Sparks of his own essence (335).

Envisioning earthly existence as a school based on the trials and tribulations of life is an alternative view about the nature of leadership and consistent with the attitude of the leaders portrayed in this book. What I have described as their ability to *navigate on the basis of a reality beyond the horizon* has developmental implications in the ongoing exploration of possibility and its integration, that is, "the proper action of Mind and Heart on each other for the purpose of forming the Soul." Not unlike the orientation provided in Goethe's line: "formation, transformation/eternal mind's eternal recreation" (79), the work of leadership draws consciously upon the imagination to continually bring forth unrealized potential, an apt description of the self-transforming mind engaged in the practice of soul-making on a collective scale.

The Transcendent Function in Organizational Life

The soul of an organization is the source of its humanity, and not unlike what happens at an individual level, the dynamic processes of transformation and growth become thwarted through a lack of interiority. The corporate self-knowledge required to release the forces of spontaneous growth means an encounter with what shapes the collective sense of meaning or purpose of an organization. This occurs naturally enough in the tension generated by a changing external environment and the basic, internal operating assumptions held in place by an organization's culture. The mental boundaries of culture are used for inclusion (who gets admitted, promoted, and excommunicated), establishing taboos (what is not permitted because it is a threat to the survival of the organization), and directing behavior (determining the parameters for the rules of engagement with others). In this way, culture operates like an immune system that establishes and reinforces norms that have proven helpful to the successful adaptation of the organization to its environment. In other words, culture is the means of self-regulation and central to a collective sense of identity... but it is based on the past. As Edgar Schein pointed out, "to learn something new in this realm requires us to resurrect, reexamine, and possibly change some of the more stable portions of our cognitive structure... such learning is intrinsically difficult because the reexamination of basic assumptions temporarily destabilizes our cognitive and interpersonal world, releasing large quantities of basic anxiety" (22).

The challenge of adaptation is evolving the principles for organizing experience (meaning-making), consistent with the demands of a more complex environment. Therefore, there is a need for members of any collective or group *to experience the limitations, inadequacies, or incomplete-*

ness of its current worldview or shared picture of reality. The trick is to do so within a degree of tolerance that the underlying assumptions of the culture (call them commitments, beliefs, or values) don't counteract or undermine efforts at releasing unrealized potential held captive by an existing immune system. Understanding that such basic assumptions even exist, among a critical mass of group members, is key to greater interiority and the ability to move from being subject to such assumptions (unaware of their influence) to witnessing or observing them and the role they play in individual and collective behavior. The differentiator is the degree of personal and collective objectivity that exists, because as Schein noted, large amounts of stress are going to result.

In my experience working with leaders in organizations of various sizes around the world, I have found that every organization has two distinct voices: public and private. The public is the voice of the business or mission that uses essentially a technical language unique to the work of the organization (e.g., markets, customers, products, services, projects, revenues, costs). The private is the voice of the organization that is essentially the language of narrative or stories told and retold within and across different functions, departments, and regions connecting members of the organization to common and shared experiences. Together, these voices comprise the tangible and intangible artifacts of the organization's culture. How these voices shape an organization can be modeled as interdependent architectures. As Figure 6.1 indicates, the public architecture charts the direction, structure, and management practices of the organization and comprises the espoused strategy, systems, and resources necessary to accomplish its goals – future action oriented. The element titled espoused strategy is concerned with the purpose and direction of the organization and seeks to clarify the vision, values, principles, and objectives that will serve as formal reference points.

Figure 1 – The Voice of Business: Public Architecture

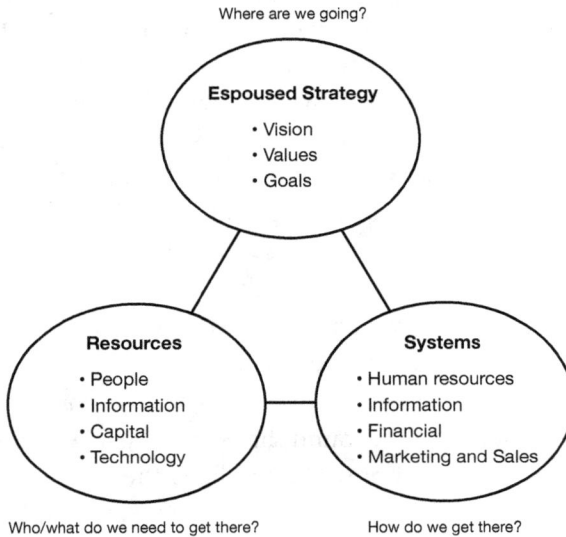

Where are we going?

Espoused Strategy
- Vision
- Values
- Goals

Resources
- People
- Information
- Capital
- Technology

Systems
- Human resources
- Information
- Financial
- Marketing and Sales

Who/what do we need to get there?   How do we get there?

The element titled systems is concerned with the structure and governance of the organization and seeks to define the decision-making processes that will guide operations. The element titled resources is focused on the support requirements for deploying the organization's strategy. No element can exist in isolation from the others. A strategy is coherent and consistent only to the degree that the various systems and resources also exist to support the strategy and vice versa. One element in non-alignment with the others results in a performance gap that, if continued, leads to a competitive lapse.

The private architecture, on the other hand, informs the nature of the interrelationships among the members of the organization and, to some degree, stakeholders who identify with the organization (e.g., contractors, customers, benefactors, investors, partners). The private architecture has its own logic constructed to underscore among the members "why things are the way they are" – past action oriented. The result of this understanding becomes evident in the "personality" or "character" of the organization - the unique combinations of competence, attitudes, and preferences within and across different aspects of organizational life. For example, there are differences between those actors (departments or individuals) operating more externally with customers or suppliers versus those operating exclusively with others inside the organization. Similarly there are differences between those actors working within what is considered the critical functions versus those working in the support functions. However, it is the way these differences add up that comprises the personality of the organization.

In Figure 6.2, the element titled perspectives illustrates the distinctive worldview of the organization, a more or less collective understanding of reality which can be broken down further in terms of sub-cultures within the organization. The element titled context focuses on the behavior and the practices that are reinforced within the organization, which again, varies across sub-cultures. If we take the position that most behaviors are learned, then context illustrates how the learning takes place. The last element is capabilities. While the other two elements can be illustrated without inferring value judgments, by its very nature this element requires a defined standard of excellence for purposes of evaluation.

Figure 2 – The Voice of Organization: Private Architecture

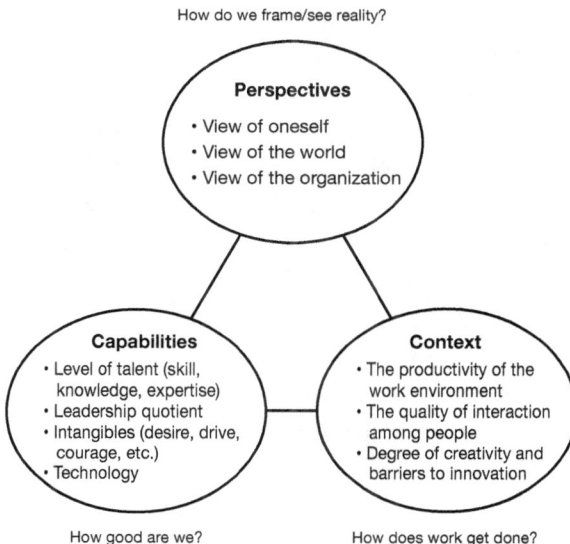

How do we frame/see reality?

Perspectives
• View of oneself
• View of the world
• View of the organization

Capabilities
• Level of talent (skill, knowledge, expertise)
• Leadership quotient
• Intangibles (desire, drive, courage, etc.)
• Technology

Context
• The productivity of the work environment
• The quality of interaction among people
• Degree of creativity and barriers to innovation

How good are we?   How does work get done?

Alignment of the two architectures does not imply the elimination of tension between competing values, goals, or objectives. Rather, alignment means creating the proper tension to balance diversity with unity, the past with the future, global thinking with local action, and collective interests with individual needs. However, even this is misleading because organizations are dynamic entities existing within a dynamic environment. In other words, the principles for organizing experience, on an individual and collective level, must continually evolve relative to the complexity of the external environment in order to adapt a shared picture of reality. This is an endless task and haphazard at best, as illustrated in Figure 6.3, yet in the absence of adaptation a deeper disturbance grows between what is essentially the "conscious state of existence" (what organizational leaders tend to direct attention toward) and the source of energy or life within an organization (a sense of purpose and connectedness). What often begins, therefore, as a minor irritant can become a serious health hazard if left unaddressed – the result of tension that has grown out of balance.

To address the dissonance resulting from the loss of soul (i.e., meaning or purpose) a critical mass of members must directly confront the disturbance in the organizational psyche caused by the limits of their shared picture of reality. Naturally enough, individuals who are in a defensive state of mind will assume a defensive posture in addressing issues of their own self-limiting beliefs, their fears or biases toward change, and their leadership capability. It is truly the unusual individual who is willing to be open and vulnerable when suspicion and cynicism pervade an organization. When trust degrades (the usual ingredient necessary to support self-objectivity), the leaders in an organization lose the means to question their own assumptions or shared picture of reality and, thus, lose the means for empathy and compassion. Absent within the life of the organization is the reflective space for individuals to (1) address the source of tension generated by the limitation of an existing worldview, (2) gain a new perspective on themselves and the world around them, and (3) develop the required capabilities to support themselves within a different context (changes in the public architecture).

Figure 3 – The Challenge to High Performing Organizations in a Dynamic Environment

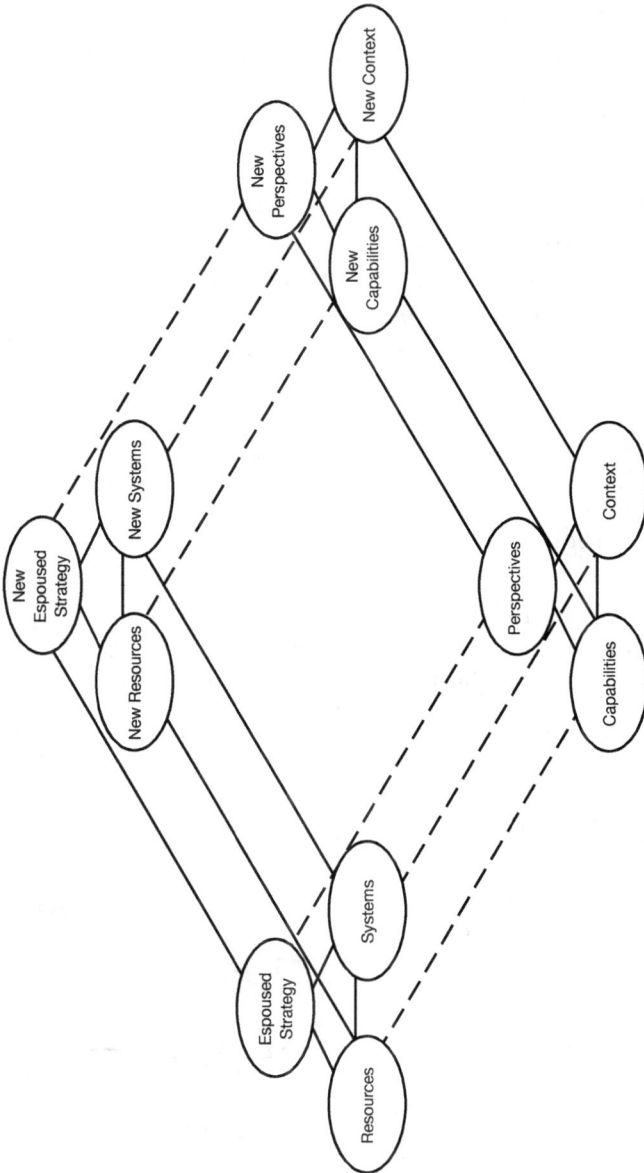

Rather than resolution through breakdown and likely removal of current leadership in favor of a new team who outside stakeholders believe will "revive the fortunes of the organization," another option is development of a "third space" within the public and private architectures of the organization. The objective is to generate a quality of dialogue supportive of the transcendence of differences rather than become an act of assimilation in "converting" the non-conformists. I call that adaptive learning, when the goal is not merely short-term economic or operational improvement but long-term sustainability through a shift in consciousness, a change in attitude, an outgrowing of an older way of life. In effect, it means a collective ability to work for the purpose of transformation and growth.

Adaptive learning, as illustrated in Figure 6.4, serves as a transcendent function in bridging the objectives of the organization and the hopes and fears of its members. The result is engagement with a legitimate interior voice in a manner necessary to reconnect individuals to their source of energy and, thus, gives rise to new horizons that revitalize the work they do.

Figure 4 – Organization Capacity Building Practice as a Transcendant Function

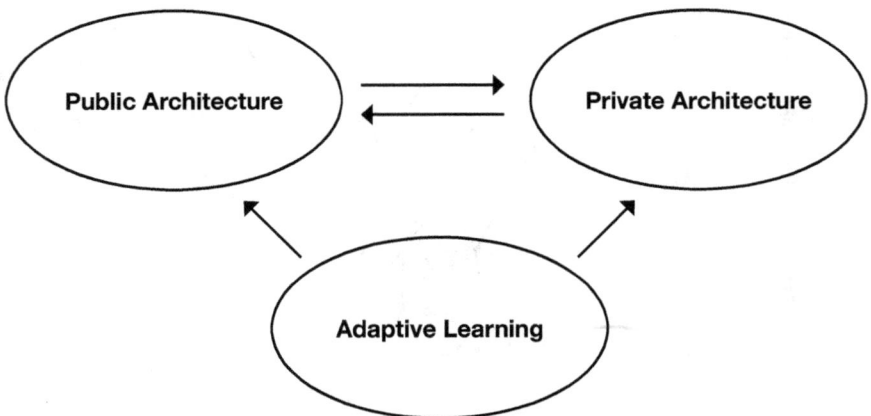

There is controversy, however, in the idea of such a function operating on a collective level. When Jung developed the concept, it was based on his experience working with patients in addressing seemingly inexplicable inner disturbances in their lives. He found it useful to their psychological growth and, as such, it became a cornerstone to his work in supporting what he referred to as the individuation process. As one Jungian scholar noted:

> Much of Jung's work stresses that through the transcendent function of the psyche, thesis and antithesis encounter one another on equal terms and achieve a symbolic synthesis that transcends them both. It is a psychological dynamic of great significance as it provides a valuable tool in overcoming sterility during conflicts and one-sided or narrow-minded points of reference. Furthermore the transcendent function becomes even more powerful if we attend to the symbols from the unconscious in an active way, and it becomes essential if we are to become committed to the goal of individuation and self-completion (Gallardo 5).

The resolution of one-sidedness is exactly the point, however, in addressing the challenge of adaptation on a collective level and not just within the psychological makeup of an individual since one-sidedness tends to result from actions taken in the past that, in effect, produce a bias for the familiar or what is already known. Such actions are ritualized through the stories and practices that emerge from the critical events in the life of a group and are passed on to new employees or group members as the unspoken rules of the organization or basic underlying assumptions. Assumptions have value to the degree that they continue to provide guidance useful to organization survival, but given the speed of change in the world, basic assumptions must be a point of inquiry on an ongoing basis within a practice that can support the necessary personal and collective objectivity to address the anxiety that will be released. This is the art of leadership, whether formal or informal. As one leader in my study described her work, "it is to create an environment for people to experience themselves as fully as possible." This means calling into question operating assumptions that may not have "tolerated" a larger vision of people (Beatrice).

The listening function of leadership, in choosing to become attuned to the interior organizational voice, begins at a personal level. The leaders I have profiled are nuanced observers of their own inner life as an ongoing practice. The transcendent function applies to them personally and is instrumental in developing inner guidance, as they often talked about it. Through their development of multiple intelligences (perceptual acuity), they consciously attend to the different ways of knowing across the spectrum of knowledge. Whether in silent meditation, inner reflection and dialogue, or engagement with others, there is "continual listening for the inspiration about what needs to be said" (Peter). In transcending self-limiting beliefs through the process of soul-making, new personal horizons emerge and with them a "shifting of the emotional centre towards loving and harmonious affections, towards 'yes, yes,' and away from 'no,' where the claims of the non-ego are concerned," as previously noted by William James (194). To make the point more explicitly, the guidance behind Mother Teresa's words to the audience of business leaders lay in the example of her own life. It is an example I also found in my experience with the leaders I spent time with. To note again, in the words of Margaret:

> There is so much unfolding still to occur, so much to learn, so much to experience. Every day I live my life there is some new learning, some new feeling to share, some new insight to pass along, some new challenge to grab hold of, and so much love.

Such a claim does not arise out of a defensive posture, but rather from the invitation that love offers as the antidote to fear, even as there will be those who scoff, dismiss as naïve, or reject what asks a vulnerability they are not ready for. Without such awareness of what whole-heartedness requires, there is no means to create the space for adaptive learning and, thereby, shift orientations. It is the practice of mindfulness that builds the capability to enlarge one's field of vision upon which the world opens up.

Mindfulness in Leadership

The concept of mindfulness is often linked to a specific state of awareness, but I would take it further to suggest it has to do with more fully awakening to who we are as individuals. To say that how we think informs our path to action is to note the importance of our state of mind in how we experience self and others. Take, for example, the following story. When the CEO of major global corporation landed at a private airfield in a large metropolitan city in the US and was not met by the driver who was expected to be there, he grew angry at the delay this was going to cause in his schedule. Even though the driver had been informed of the plane's landing time and location, he became confused due to the close proximity of two private airports and showed up at the wrong location. When the driver became aware of his mistake, he made great haste to get to the correct airfield. The CEO became increasingly angry as he waited. Fortunately, he had an extraordinary leader with him on that trip. When she observed the unsettled state of mind of her CEO and heard the comments he was making about firing the driver as soon as he arrived, she made a quick assessment of the situation and replied: "Whatever you say to this man when he shows up you will quickly forget soon afterwards, but he will remember it for the rest of his life." The comment caught him by surprise, for in his reactive anger to an unexpected event he had become mindless about the consequences of the influence he had - a dangerous precedent for any leader, as he quickly realized and changed his attitude about the turn of events that day.

How we think encompasses multiple lines of development under the umbrella of mental functioning. What that entails is illustrated in the Ladder of Inference, which is based on the work of a number of psychologists and organizational theorists, particularly Chris Argyris (Tompkins and Rhodes 84-85). In Figure 6.5, the model illustrates several steps or stages from "available data" to "take action." In total, movement across these steps is a function of a current state of development along each of an individual's cognitive, emotional, moral, intrapersonal, and interpersonal lines of development.

As Argyris argued, human beings are present to an immense amount of data from which we organize "all propositions [we hold] about the structure and operation of society" (6). In other words, to function within our respective contexts we filter or screen the available data based on our life experiences, education, interests, aptitudes, and other formative influences that contribute to the creation of our internal operating system – the intrapersonal line of development.

Figure 6.5 – The Ladder of Inference

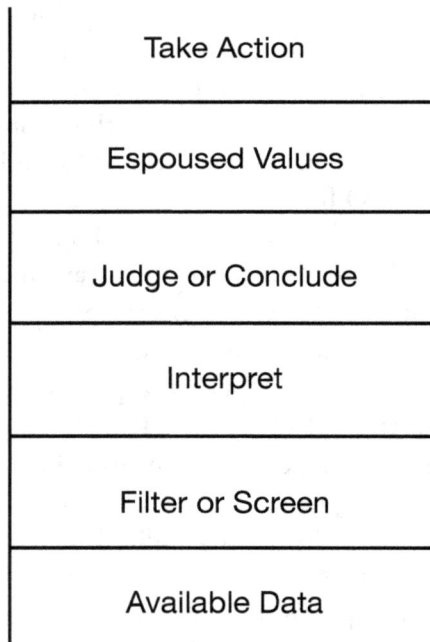

| Take Action |
| Espoused Values |
| Judge or Conclude |
| Interpret |
| Filter or Screen |
| Available Data |

Our filters, or what Argyris called "theories-in-use," are often unconscious and triggered quickly in reaction to situations we face (6). These reactions are first perceived at the interpret stage of the ladder and experienced on an emotional level as something we find enjoyable, fearful, distasteful, embarrassing, inspiring, exciting, etc. We don't yet fully understand our response until the next level of the ladder when we come to a conclusion or judgment about the situation we face. Here we translate feelings into meaning, on a cognitive level, and rationalize our response in a pronouncement leading to action. The words we use to justify our actions (our espoused values) are an attempt to align our moral and interpersonal dimensions. Reactive tendencies show up as particular patterns of behavior - what I refer to as "personal success strategies" - in meeting the urgent demands of our context. The shadow side of our reactive tendencies is the way we rush up the Ladder of Inference, often to the detriment of learning, which limits our adaptive capacity.

Adaptive learning requires both openness to our experience without jumping to conclusions and the willingness to allow the imagination to come into play (the very means of surfacing the assumptions embedded in our internal operating system without succumbing to anxiety). This is what I understand non-judgmental inquiry to mean, which has become a core element in the definition of mindfulness. Jon Kabat-Zinn, creator of the Mindfulness Based Stress Reduction program at the University of Massachusetts School of Medicine, wrote, "Mindfulness means paying attention in a particular way: on purpose, in the present moment, and non-judgmentally" (3). To inquire non-judgmentally is not just a critical approach to knowledge, as implied by scientific inquiry, but embraces a playfulness based on the concept of leisure or contemplation. By linking the two words – leisure and contemplation – I am noting a catalytic relationship. Contemplation requires a discipline of mind that is not reactive to events around us, but is deliberate in increasing mental complexity through cleansing the doors of perception. It is a practice and a way of life.

Josef Pieper, a 20th century scholastic philosopher, noted that "leisure is not the attitude of mind of those who actively intervene but of those who are open to everything; not of those who grab hold but of those who leave the reins loose and are free and easy themselves..." (47). The word for leisure in Latin is scola from which the English word school (and scholasticism) derives. Similarly, the word for play in Latin is ludum which means the place of elementary education. To be at leisure

– at school – is to be open to surprise, to allow something new to arise, to expect the unexpected for the shift of attitude or expanded state of consciousness that will result. It is the way "to assure that we, embedded in our social function [of work], are enabled to remain fully human. That we may not lose the ability to look beyond the limits of our social and functional station, to contemplate and celebrate the world as such, to become and be that person who is essentially oriented toward the whole of reality" (Pieper 49).

Mindfulness as a practice of awakening to the fullness of Self means (1) presence or openness to each moment with an ever widening field of awareness, (2) the self-knowledge sufficient to experience the feelings or emotions that arise without critique, and (3) the personal objectivity not to be overwhelmed by what is triggered by conditioning from formative influences (i.e., underlying assumptions). This is why mindfulness as a contemplative practice is relevant to the work of leadership. It is not easy to be an observer and participant simultaneously when situations call into question our own beliefs or convictions. And yet this observation mode is necessary to take the position of others, to let in alternative perspectives, and to experience the tension that occurs without rushing to judgment. It begins with what the neurologist, Daniel Sigel, called "widening our window of tolerance:"

> Think of the window as the band of arousal (of any kind) within which an individual can function well. This band can be narrow or wide. If an experience pushes us outside our window of tolerance, we may fall into rigidity and depression on the one hand, or into chaos on the other. In our day-to-day experience, we have multiple windows of tolerance. And for each of us those windows are different, often specific to certain topics or certain emotional states. I may have a high tolerance for sadness, continuing to function fairly well even when I or those around me are in deep distress. But even a lesser degree of sadness – whether your own or others' – may cause you to fall apart. In contrast, anger may be relatively intolerable for me; a raised voice may be enough to send me right out my narrow window.

But for you, anger may not be such a big deal; you see a blowup as a way to "clear the air" and move on... Within our window of tolerance we remain receptive; outside of it we become reactive... In many cases our well-being depends on widening the window of tolerance so that we can hold the elements of our internal world in awareness – without being thrown into rigidity (depression, cutoffs, avoidance) or chaos (agitation, anxiety, rage)... (137-138).

What encourages the playfulness that widens the window of tolerance in the face of uncertainty? As Siegel noted:

The presence of a caring, trusted other person, one who is attuned to our internal world, is often the initial key to widening our windows of tolerance. . . Here is a key fact about relationships: The resonance circuitry not only allows us to "feel felt" and to connect with one another, but it also helps to regulate our internal state... This is how in the moment, face-to-face, we help one another grow, and initiate the long-term synaptic changes that help us even when we're apart (137-139).

Here is the point again of Mother Teresa's injunction that in creating caring relationships with others there is a mirroring function that allows them to connect with themselves, thus slowing the reactive tendency to rush up the Ladder of Inference when under duress, and thereby increasing the means for becoming more mindful.

Physicist F. David Peat created a more direct link to the practice of mindfulness when he noted the profundity of the seemingly inexplicable relationship between the brain and the mind:

For the act of thinking changes the thinker. Indeed just as there is an irreducible link between observer and observed in the quantum theory, so, within consciousness is there an irreducible link between the thinker and the thought. Indeed the thinker is the thought; the thought gives birth to the thinker who, in turn, creates the thought anew. Therefore, rather than the brain creating thought, it is thought which generates the brain. Or rather, that the brain and its activities are inseparable and through their constant activity both brain and mind are created and maintained...

One of the leading researchers on neural networks, Eric Kandel, has written: ... even during simple social experiences as when two people speak to each other, the action of the neuronal machinery in one person's brain is capable of having a direct and long lasting effect on the modifiable synaptic connections in the brain of the other.

... Kandel's example of the conversation provides an image of two neural networks engaged in the dance which modifies and maintains them both. Minds are the unfolding of thought. Meaning is once again discovered to be crucial in determining the world. It is the unfolding of this meaning in time which produces the whole gesture of the mind's dance. Within this gesture, brain and consciousness are sustained just as the fountain lives by virtue of the water that flows through it (108-9).

To describe minds as "the unfolding of thought" implies that truth doesn't exist in objects, but rather in the way we know. Meaning, as Peat observed, is how we experience the life around us and the life within us.

This brings us back to the experiences of the leaders in this book and the development of their orientation to what gets labeled as "reality." Simply stated, leaders have one of two choices in addressing the increasing complexity of the modern world; either they confine their exposure to what is familiar (what they already believe they understand) or they build their inner complexity to meet the outer complexity they encounter (what is unfamiliar, other, foreign, or unknown). The latter entails creating the space to be present (mindful) with what challenges inner stability and meaning in a playful and compassionate manner. It is its own end, but practically speaking, it is the means for emergent thinking, innovation, and transformation. To be more literal, exploration and integration are the two halves of a mindfulness practice for consciously engaging in transformation. This practice begins to anticipate the tipping points where shifts in worldviews are possible and provide the means for more agile navigation of the transition.

Exploration is a directed process of acquiring greater self-knowledge. It takes on different tactics depending on the stage of one's development but, in essence, it is built on reflection, introspection, and meditation. At the heart of a practice of mindfulness is a personal relationship with one's self. What are the nuances of self, soul, and/or spirit? For what reasons do we exist? What can we know? These are more than speculative questions because how they are answered will directly shape one's focus, attention, effort, commitment, and perseverance. In other words, performance is a matter of self-knowledge. While exploration intends to break through self-limiting beliefs, integration intends to build insight into the life we are given. The peak experience associated with expanded states of awareness is not uncommon, but it is not a gift to be taken lightly. If action is not taken to carry our insights back into the world of everyday existence, we risk losing them to the unconscious.

Integration is the practice of translation and application. Just as exploration widens one's field of vision, thus enabling the emergence of something new, integration results in a set of implications for future action. Meaning-making or mental functioning includes the way we solve problems, make decisions, and interact with others. Therefore, personal development leading to an evolution of one's internal navigation system requires the challenge of daily existence. To embrace our freedom means to make choices. How we frame our choices, act upon them, and live with the consequences is indicative of our adaptation to the context of our life. Mindfulness is to view our lives as experiments in fulfilling our potential. We strive for self-realization and in that striving all data is friendly. We learn as much by what we didn't expect as by what we did, which returns us to exploration and the new questions that have arisen. This cycle of growth and development leads to greater self-observation skills in an ever-widening spiral of action – reflection – conceptualization – implication – action. Exceptional leadership therefore begins with being present to the mystery of life, experiencing it in the depth of our own souls, and translating that insight through the choices we each are called to make.

As a final example, I share the story of a man who returns from war psychologically shaken, his marriage in disarray, and with little motivation to pursue his career aspirations. He has recently become more troubled by dreams that have begun to haunt him throughout his waking hours. He is distracted, unable to focus, and his spirit is failing. One day he sees his physician, with whom he has been confiding his fears and dark forebodings. This older man is a good listener, kind, and true to the troubled young man. The physician often tells him things that help to calm his nerves and today the young man hopes for more of the same. After sharing the way his nightly visitations had begun to show up randomly in the course of his day as frightening visions, the older man surprises him with his interpretation of events, "If you're frightened of dying and you're holding on you'll see devils tearing your life away. But if you've made your peace, then the devils are really angels freeing you from the earth" (Rubin 82).

To navigate on the basis of what lies beyond the horizon is only possible with the knowledge that what is helping to free us from the attitudes to which we have become captive is that aspect of our Self that is intimate with transformation. Unless we are weaned from self-limiting beliefs and fears, we eventually stand to lose that which we are desperately trying to protect – our sense of purpose or meaning. And therein lies the great paradox that all spiritual teachers have referenced in one way or another; we must lose ourselves in order to find ourselves. But what feels like death is in fact a birthing process, and the transition from one state of existence to the next is the fundamental drama of life. As Joseph Campbell wrote:

> no matter what the stage or grade of life, the call rings up the curtain, always on a mystery of transfiguration — a rite or moment, of spiritual passage, which, when complete, amounts to a dying and a birth. The familiar life horizon has been outgrown; the old concepts,

ideals, and emotional patterns no longer fit; the time for the passing of a threshold is at hand (*The Hero with a Thousand Faces* 51).

Transformation is the path we walk in our personal journey. To the degree we work in alignment with this journey, it does feel like "angels" are helping us along. And with that acceptance comes the experience of whole-heartedness, which these leaders referenced, in their own way, as the gift of soul work.

Epilogue

There is no way to give people purpose and principles,
nor can there be self-governance without them. The only possibility
is to evoke the gift of self-governance from the people to themselves.

Dee Hock

THE EVOLUTIONARY ARROW that runs through life will not be broken by vandals, raiders, or self-proclaimed saviors, even though such people do exist. The story of human existence will continue to unfold in ways we have yet to imagine, but then that is the point. In a follow-up conversation five years later with several of the leaders in my study, I found they were growing in ways they had not imagined. Their lives continued to be a source of mystery even as others sought them out for guidance and instruction. It is one of the paradoxes they found particularly humorous. On the one hand, they were aware of their growth and the responsibility that comes with how they choose to share their gifts with others. On the other hand, they knew their limitations. As Frank noted, "you build a construct and then you have to take it apart." It was his way of saying that whatever map or model guides his leadership journey, inevitably at some point it must be rebuilt. This is "the gathering of wisdom which allows a perspective on the journey." One such lesson he now carries is "the meaning of nuance - the bittersweet. Results are not always what you expected, but there is always a gift that comes with it."

The drive towards wholeness, as opposed to perfection, is learning to admit that the other's perspective matters. This other is whoever or whatever we have yet to achieve a reconciliation, whether that is with some aspect of ourselves we have broken off and disavowed or another person who stands apart from us that we have labeled foreign, different, or strange. In either case, there is adaptive learning yet to be done to liberate our unrealized life. I call the people in my study leaders because they have been bound by fears born of wounds they did not understand and, yet, found a way to show compassion towards themselves. They are leaders because they learned to offer that way of wholeness in their interactions with others. It is learning to walk in a manner that regards all life as sacred. And in that declaration is the recognition we all come from a single source and a prior unity. To know this means to honor that source in each person. Self-governance (soul work) is the natural extension of this way of leading, but with a difference for the leaders in my study. As previously noted in Dee Hock's story, regardless of how willing people were to be engaged by the openness, the freedom, and the trust that had been created, many felt these characteristics applied "to them in relation to those to whom they reported, but not in relation to those over whom they reported" (276). The degree of continual growth and development is easily underestimated for self-governance to operate on a collective level. To understand this point is to understand the need for self-transforming leaders who can evoke the gift of self-governance from others towards themselves without demanding it.

The practice that Regina expressed in my conversation with her was one of "finding the balance between concentrating and relaxing, between offering my gifts as a leader to others and letting go of my gifts." It is a practice of opening up and taking in without critical thought and then narrowing one's focus on what has been received and taking action. This opening-focusing cycle, used consciously, has deepened Regina's engagement with her inner guidance on a real-time basis, as situations require. The importance of this practice to self-governance is to realize that leadership, like any art, is based on inspiration.

Warren Bennis has said, "the leader's work is inner work" (1989), meaning of course that developing a relationship with one's own source of guidance is the means for not only a rich inner life but greater nuance in responding to the complexity of the external environment. To not overreach in pursuit of one's vision is to recognize that what we offer as leaders must be tested with the source of the inspiration behind that vision. That's a continual process of "checking-in," best illustrated through a story told by a poet who was once asked how he went about writing a poem. He began at night in a room at the top of his house while below him his family slept. The silence of his home evoked a meditative state where images would flow into his mind. He would sketch them in words as quickly as possible. Over the next several days or weeks he would apply his art as a writer to shape these initial images into a poem. But before he would share the poem with others he would return to his room atop the house at night and offer it to the source of his inspiration by asking, "Is this what is meant to be said?" An inner dialogue would follow that guided his next steps to either rework the poem, publish it as is, or set off in a completely different direction.

In Olivia's case, her creative entrepreneurial talents, not unlike the poet's, have always been a source of joy. However, rather than expressing her passions in words, she expresses them addressing needs she felt she could do something about. "My latent energies get activated when I see something in the world I want to change." Her visionary skills, what she described as foresight, developed along with her ability "to continuously keep my ego at bay." How she went about doing that was both a part of her spiritual development – noting that she was merely attuning to what the universe had in store for her – and creating the container around her vision that acts like a clarion call. "People begin to show up who want to apply their talents in support of a vision that inspires them. And they do things I could never have imagined."

The output of soul work is translating what exists beyond the horizon in bringing forth more life to our daily existence. It begins with imagination and a desire to explore the unknown, as illustrated by the leaders in this book. They developed a trust in finding that place where identity dissolves in order for something new to emerge, what they described as being in a liminal space. Here is where their source of guidance would meet them and out of which their relationship with inner guidance was forged. It was a playground that allowed them to let go of the concerns of their worldly existence, which carried over into a playful attitude towards life generally. But even more, they discovered the empathic force within themselves that was always ever present. And in that way, they learned the nature of compassion, which guides their work as leaders in creating environments that "widen the windows of tolerance" necessary for evoking the gift of self-governance from the people to themselves.

Attachment 1

Phase I of a Study on the Effects of Long-Term Participation in The Monroe Institute Programs

THE MONROE INSTITUTE (TMI), through its patented sound technology, has demonstrated changes in focused states of consciousness for thousands of individuals over the last 35 years (Russell 105). While ongoing research at the Institute on the nature of different states of consciousness is yielding rich insights into human development, a continuing challenge for the leadership of TMI is to understand how repeated exposure to Hemi-Sync® technology in controlled workshop environments affects the quality of individual lives. Does it have any bearing on the degree of self-efficacy, life satisfaction, job satisfaction, and career performance? In other words, does repeated exposure to TMI programs increase the capacity of the participants to deal with the demands of their lives in terms of doing meaningful work, developing and supporting mutually rewarding relationships, and in acquiring skills and attitudes that provoke continual growth and development?

A second challenge for the long-term benefit of the Institute is to attract participation in graduate level programs. While the workshops are well structured and the experience of participants during these workshops well documented, the percentage of individuals involved with TMI over 3 or more years remains fairly low. Data suggests there is a 30-month window from the time individuals first hear of TMI to the time their interest in the Institute wanes. In that time individuals will often participate in 1-3 programs. After that time, participation dwindles significantly. Why is that? Clearly, the benefits of additional programs, once individuals have satisfied some intrinsic need that brought them to the Institute to begin with, are not well understood nor promoted as part of the Institute's mission.

To address these challenges, a study was proposed to look at the long-term effects of participation in TMI programs. An online survey was developed on the following dimensions:

- Demographics (6 items) – gender, age, education, income, race
- Psychographics (19 items) – job status & transition, family status & transition, number of programs attended, personal objectives for attendance, support or resistance to attendance from family members and/or friends, continuing contact with TMI alumni and facilitators, memorable moments from the program(s), etc.
- Program Effects (36 items) – decision making effectiveness, outlook on life, interaction with others, job & career satisfaction, stress management, alignment of actions with personal values, work-life balance, ongoing personal development, etc.
- Keirsey-Bates Temperament Sorter (optional – 70 items) – assessing personality characteristics

The study looked at 2 groups of individuals:

- Those who have attended only the Gateway program, the entry level program, and hereafter referred to a GO (Gateway Only)
- Those who have attended three or more programs and hereafter referred to as MP (Multiple Programs)

The online survey was distributed to each group via a letter of invitation from the President of TMI. There were 385 responses from GO and 341 responses from MP. The average response for all items on the survey was 366 for GO and 328 for MP. The N population when combining both groups was 694 in Table 2 – Means, Standard Deviations, and Correlations and further broken down by specific item (see appendix). The population for this study was taken from the TMI database which was automated in 2000. Participants were all found in the automated version which means they had taken at least one program since 2000. Those with attendance at three or more programs included programs dating back to the late 1970s.

Organization of the Findings

Given the number of responses and the number and types of questions in the survey, there is a wealth of data that has not been fully mined. The principle objective in this report is to address the primary question of long-term effects both statistically and qualitatively. The findings are divided into four sections:

- Section 1 - Comparison of responses for selected items within the demographic and psychographics section and the results of an independent analysis of the data
- Section 2 - Keirsey-Bates Temperament Sorter (KBTS) results compared with a national norm base and the results of an independent analysis of the data
- Section 3 - Factor and regression analysis of the program effects data controlled for the variables identified in the demographic and KBTS results together with a comparison of responses for selected items
- Section 4 - Qualitative review of comments to an open-ended item describing the most memorable experience at TMI and concluding comments

To jump to the punch line, there is statistically significant evidence suggesting clear differences in terms of self-efficacy and life satisfaction between the GO and the MP groups. This is further corroborated by a comparison of comments from respondents about their experiences at TMI where the quality and frequency of references to life changes are different for those having attended three or more programs.

One qualification regarding the data; for those in the group designated MP, the assumption that three programs is the cut-off for the majority of respondents is not accurate. In fact, based on those who did respond to the question of how many programs they have attended, more than 75%

had attended "four or more programs." That is significant in terms of program effects, however, it is difficult to determine what, if any, difference is a result of having attending three or four or even how many respondents had attended more than four programs.

Section 1 – Demographic & Psychographics Analysis

As the database only includes participants who have attended a TMI program since the year 2000 there are no GO participants prior to that year included in this survey. It isn't the same story for the MP respondents. While they have had to attend a program since 2000 to be in the database, there are examples in the survey of individuals who attended programs in the 1970s and 80s. This would be one reason why respondents who have attended multiple programs have a higher percentage in the 56-60 and 61-70 age brackets.

Age	Percentage of MP Respondents	Percentage of GO Respondents
21-25	0	3.07
26-30	1.92	3.83
31-35	4.21	4.98
36-40	5.75	9.2
41-45	7.66	10.34
46-50	16.48	16.09
51-55	23.37	23.75
56-60	19.92	15.71
61-70	15.71	9.96
70+	4.98	3.07

A characteristic of the MP respondents is their higher degree of curiosity and desire for self-knowledge. This is evident in their reasons for attending TMI illustrated in the table below. From among the list of choices, respondents were instructed to indicate all that applied to them.

The two choices that clearly indicated a difference between the 2 groups were "curiosity" and "understanding myself better" (together with "learn new skills" which was marginally higher).

"My reasons for attending TMI were":	Percentage of MP Respondents	Percentage of GO Respondents
Curiosity	65.48	56.2
Understanding myself better	63.1	53.3
Solve a problem or issue in my life	16.07	17.94
Rejuvenation and renewal	27.68	26.91
Recommendation from another	22.62	26.91
Learn new skills	51.79	47.23
Part of a professional development plan	7.14	5.01
Part of a personal development plan	41.67	39.31
Other	24.4	21.11

Further to the point of distinction between the 2 populations, it is not surprising to see a higher percentage of MP respondents have advanced degrees. Half of the MP respondents (48.8 %) have a Masters, Doctoral, or Professional degree, whereas for GO respondents it is significantly less (37.9%).

Education	Percentage of MP Respondents	Percentage of GO Respondents
Less than high school	0	0.77
High School/ GED	3.08	6.51
Some College	13.85	14.18
2 – Year Degree (Associates)	6.15	9.58
Bachelor Degree	28.85	31.03
Masters Degree	25.38	23.37
Doctoral Degree	13.08	7.28
Professional Degree (MD, JD)	9.62	7.28

With a slightly higher proportion of respondents in the 56 – 70 age range and a higher proportion of advanced and professional degree holders, it is also no surprise to find a higher percentage of MP respondents earning $70,000 +. More than half of the MP respondents (53.26%) earn $70,000 or more annually compared with just four out of ten (40.61%) of the GO respondents.

Income	Percentage of MP Respondents	Percentage of GO Respondents
< $30,000	15.33	21.46
$30K – 49,999	14.18	20.31
$50K – 69,999	17.24	17.62
$70K – 99,999	24.9	18.39
$100K – 149,999	11.88	12.26
$150K – 199,999	6.9	3.83
$200K – $300,000	3.83	2.68
More than $300,000	5.75	3.45

Once again, given the higher percentage of respondents in the 61-70 and 71+ age categories it is no surprise to find that a statistically significantly higher percentage of MP respondents are retired. Nonetheless, the percentage still in the workforce is quite comparable between the 2 groups. Of interest is the statistically significant high unemployment rate in the GO respondents. A contributing factor could be the higher percentage of younger people in this group. To speculate, a higher percentage of participants could have been students and in the absence of such a category they chose to indicate that they were unemployed.

Employment	Percentage of MP Respondents	Percentage of GO Respondents
Unemployed	1.57	11.24
Self-Employed	47.45	44.57
Employed	35.29	34.88
Retired	15.69	9.3

One final focus of analysis is the civil status of the participants. Given the high percentage of respondents who are married the difference between the two groups is not statistically significant. However, given the smaller percentage of respondents who are single the difference between the two groups is statistically significant. The same is marginally true for the percentage of respondents who are widowed. However, there is not a significant difference between the total percentage of respondents who are separated, divorced, or widowed. Nonetheless, GO respondents have a significantly larger percentage separated, divorced or widowed in the 3-5 year window whereas MP respondents have a significantly larger percentage separated, divorced or widowed 6 years or longer (see the second table below).

Civil Status	Percentage of MP Respondents	Percentage of GO Respondents
Single	17.05	21.24
Married	54.65	51.74
Separated	3.1	4.25
Divorced	20.93	20.46
Widowed	4.26	2.32

If Separated, Divorced, or Widowed, for How Long?	Percentage of MP Respondents	Percentage of GO Respondents
< 1 Year	2.56	4.57
1–2 Years	3.59	4.11
3-5 Years	7.18	12.79
6-10 Years	13.33	10.5
> 10 years	30.26	24.2

The few key differences noted above were also verified by an independent statistical analysis of all responses:

Characteristic	Difference
Gender	N.S.
Age	GO younger
Employment	GO more unemployed MP more retired
Education	MP more educated
Individual Income	MP higher
Partner Income	N.S.
Marital status	GO significantly more single MP marginally more widowed
Time married / cohabitating	N.S.
Time divorced / widowed	MP more years divorced or separated
Race	GO has more Hispanics

Key: GO = Gateway Only Sample;
MP = Multiple Programs Sample;
N.S. = no significant difference

With these differences noted, some general comments can be made about the target audience for TMI from a combined profile of both groups. Individuals who come to TMI are as likely to be a man as a woman, they are slightly more likely to be married as single/separated/ divorced/widowed, slightly more than 65% will be between the ages of 41 and 60 (with the largest single percentage between the ages of 51 & 55), 69% will hold a bachelor's degree or higher, 79.5% will be employed (with 35% self-employed), 72% will be earning less than $100,000 per year, and nearly 90% will be white Caucasian.

Though this is not a market study, it warrants some observations based on the general profile of both groups. In my judgment it is no co-incidence that the largest percentage of TMI program participants comes from the 41-60 age groups. These are the age groups that have made it past mid-life and now look beyond the short-term goals that have defined their life - meeting the requirements of a job or career, taking care of a family, and building a position or role in a community. While scanning ahead is always a part of life, it isn't until a certain foundation has been laid, either in terms of personal success or failure, that a change in per-spective emerges and new questions arise from a vantage point that did not exist in one's 20s or even 30s. The new questions cannot be answered as easily or with sufficient confidence through traditional sources and so starts the process of widening a circle of inquiry that eventually leads to contact with places like TMI.

Section 2 – Keirsey-Bates Temperament Sorter Analysis

The Keirsey-Bates Temperament Sorter (KBTS) is one of several in-struments used to measure personality type preference. Modeled after the Myers-Briggs Type Indicator (MBTI), the Keirsey-Bates Temperament Sorter provides a framework for determining predispositions toward fa-vored or natural tendencies in human behavior. Both instruments seek to determine how people consciously prefer to attend to the world, how they choose to perceive that to which they attend, and how judgments are made about those perceptions.

The KBTS dimensions are based on four bipolar scales, Extraversion-Introversion, Sensing-Intuition, Thinking-Feeling, and Judging-Perceiving that are measured by a series of 10-20 responses. The questions are structured as either/or statements to a wide range of human situations to determine personal preferences. A sample of the types of questions is listed below:

1. Are visionaries
   a. somewhat annoying
   b. rather fascinating
2. Are you more comfortable with work that is
   a. contracted
   b. done on a casual basis
3. In relationships should most things be
   a. renegotiable
   b. random and circumstantial

The typology scales are comprised of 8 dimensions, which combine to create one of sixteen different personality typologies:

1. The EI Scale – The focus of attention
   - Extraversion – People who prefer extraversion tend to get their energy from others and this is where they tend to direct their energy. They need to experience the world in order to understand it and thus tend to like action.
   - Introversion – People who prefer introversion tend to get their energy from their inner world and this is where they tend to direct their energy. They like to understand the world before experiencing it and so often thing about what they are doing before acting.
2. The SN Scale – The means of acquiring information
   - Sensing – For these individuals their senses are the means for figuring out what is actually happening inside and outside of themselves. Sensing types tend to accept and work with what is "given" in the here-and-now.
   - Intuition – For these individuals there is meaning that goes beyond the information from the senses. Intuition looks at the big picture and tries to grasp the essential patterns.

3. The TF Scale – How decisions are made
   - Thinking – These individuals like to consider the logical consequences of any particular choice or action before making decisions. People with a preference for thinking seek an objective standard of truth.
   - Feeling – These individuals begin with what feels important to themselves or others and make decisions on the basis of person-centered values. When making a decision for themselves, they ask how much they care. Those with a preference for feeling like dealing with people and tend to become sympathetic, appreciative, and tactful.
4. The JP Scale – The orientation toward the outer world
   - Judgment – Those who take a judging attitude (either thinking or feeling) tend to live in a planned, orderly way, wanting to regulate life and control it. People with a preference for judging like to be structured and organized and want things settled.
   - Perception – Those who prefer a perceptive process when dealing with the outer world (either sensing or intuiting) likes to live in a flexible, spontaneous way. People with a preference for perceiving seek to understand life rather than control it.

The assignment of types is determined by the summation of the responses consistent with the poles of the respective dimensions. For example, an E score of 8 (out of 10) indicates a moderately high extravert whereas a score of 2 indicates a moderately high introvert. Note that the other three dimensions are based on 20 points.

Two points are worth stressing about the KBTS data. First, this was an optional section of the survey meant as much as an enticement for respondents to take the survey as for gathering personality typology data. A self-scoring mechanism was included with the survey for those wanting to calculate their KBTS typology. As a consequence of this optional feature there were 112 respondents who did not complete the KBTS. Second, the scale used for determining preferences on each of the 4 dimensions is an even number. The possibility exists, therefore, that respondents could fall in the middle of the scale where assignment of a specific tendency or preference becomes ambiguous. There were 164 respondents with one or more dimensions of their typology which were unassignable. This left 418 respondents whose personality typology was assigned (208 for the GO respondents and 210 for the MP respondents) which is still a robust sample size.

Overall, the two groups are similar in terms of personality on a per dimension basis. The MP group is marginally higher on extraversion. Below is a table illustrating the distribution of personality typology by global norms and for each of the populations in the study.

TYPE INDICATOR	GLOBAL NORMS	GO	MP
ESTJ	10%	3.4%	4.3%
ENTJ	3%	8.2%	8.1%
ISTP	2%	-	0.5%
INTP	3%	3.4%	1.4%
ESFJ	12%	2.4%	2.4%
ENFJ	8%	18.3%	18.6%
ISFP	3%	-	-
INFP	7%	9.1%	7.6%
ESTP	3%	-	-
ESFP	5%	-	1.0%
ISTJ	10%	7.2%	2.9%
ISFJ	10%	1.9%	3.8%
ENTP	2%	2.9%	2.9%
ENFP	8%	24.5%	26.7%
INTJ	6%	6.7%	10.5%
INFJ	8%	12.0%	9.5%
Sample Size	4,586,300	208	210

TYPE INDICATOR	GLOBAL NORMS	GO	MP
Dominant Function			
S	28%	9.1%	7.7%
N	24%	46.1%	49.5%
T	18%	15%	14.3%
F	30%	29.8%	28.5%
Auxiliary Function			
S	27%	5.8%	7.2%
N	21%	39%	35.7%
T	21%	16.8%	16.3%
F	31%	38.4%	40.8%
Source of Energy			
E	51%	59.7%	64%
I	49%	40.3%	36%
Number of Inconclusive Type Indicator		87	77

Dominant Function in the table above describes the "favorite" process allocated by type (see Table 1 in the appendix). This indicates whether the favorite preference is a perception or judgment function (sensing/intuition vs. thinking/feeling). The Auxiliary Function is the secondary preference. In personality typology language, both are needed for dealing effectively with the world. One takes the lead – a perception function (sensing or intuiting) or a judgment function (thinking or feeling) – and the other balances this orientation. Extraverts tend to direct their dominant function towards the external world and use their auxiliary function dealing with their internal world. Introverts tend to direct their dominant function towards their internal world and use their auxiliary function dealing with the external world.

TMI graduates as a group are primarily different from the global norm in terms of how they like to acquire information. They strongly depend on intuition as the means of discovery and meaning-making both as their favorite and auxiliary function. One consequence of this orientation is the value placed on imagination and inspiration, which means that TMI graduates tend to be more idealistic and less tolerant of the "way things are." Further, given their higher extraversion as a group than the general population this intolerance is more often directed to the outside world. TMI graduates have a predilection for transformational growth – the radical, vertical leaps in being as opposed to the less risky, more pragmatic, horizontal extensions of being. A challenge of this orientation is finding effective means for managing the tension between what is and what could be. To look too closely for too long at the limitations in "the way things are," particularly when tolerance is low to begin with, can create bruised sensitivities, alienation, and despair (symptoms made famous by the Romantic poets). In effect, why would people with this orientation find much to be happy about? It is a question to be returned to in the conclusion.

Section 3 – Program Effects Analysis

Program effects were measured in terms of life satisfaction, job/career satisfaction, quality of life, and overall well-being. A factor analysis of the items in this section of the survey was undertaken to group questions together into subscales based on common response patterns. The analysis determined there were four factors which demonstrated better loading patterns than three factor or five factor solutions. The four factors and their accompanying items are:

1. Personal efficacy
   - I am a more effective decision maker
   - I have a more expansive vision of how the parts of my life relate to a whole
   - I am more able to surface issues that others are reluctant to talk about
   - I am more actively involved in my own personal development

- I have a clear sense of further development I need to accomplish
- I am more composed under pressure
- I take actions that are more true to my sense of self
- I have more balance among my work, my family, and my community
- I am more able to listen nondefensively to criticism
- I am able to handle stress more effectively
- I act on my values more consistently
- I have interest in new things
- I have a more open communication with my family
- I am more productive at work
- I have developed new friends
- I have been able to resolve an important issue or challenge in my life
- I am more confident in my interaction with others
- I have a clear sense of purpose in my life

2. Life satisfaction
   - The conditions of my life are excellent
   - I am satisfied with my life
   - So far I have gotten the important things in my life
   - In most ways, my life is close to ideal

3. Job satisfaction
   - Most days I am enthusiastic about my work
   - I like my job better than the average worker does
   - I find real enjoyment in my work
   - I am fairly well satisfied with my present job

4. Career Performance
   - At work I am viewed by my supervisor as an exceptional performer
   - Compared to other people my age and who are involved in the same occupation or types of work I do, I feel that I am very successful
   - The people I work with would say that I am very successful
   - I feel that my career is progressing very well compared with my peers

Three items from the survey were eliminated either because they cross-load on two different factors or have a loading less than .05.

Scale scores were generated averaging the responses, which loaded highest on each factor. Each subscale demonstrated high internal reliability (note: alphas greater than 0.7 indicate reliable measures):

1. Personal efficacy – alpha = 0.95
2. Life satisfaction – alpha = 0.9
3. Job satisfaction – alpha = 0.91
4. Career performance – alpha = 0.83

Zero order correlations with the demographic and personality typology (KBTS) variables were computed with the four factors. Table 2 in the appendix shows the correlations in addition to the total sample available for each variable, the means, and the standard deviations. Regression analysis determined the effect of attendance in multiple TMI programs on the derived factors controlling for demographic and personality typology variables. Since the four factors highly correlated with each other, multivariate regression (which controls for the factors' common variance) was used. Two models were developed due to the fact that the KBTS was optional and there were significant differences between participants who completed these questions in the survey and those who did not. Model One (Table 3 in the appendix) excludes personality data and Model Two (Table 4 in the appendix) includes it.

Overall, the results suggest that individuals who have attended multiple TMI programs experience statistically greater personal efficacy and life satisfaction than those who only attend the Gateway program. Although increased attendance in TMI programs appears to be also associated with greater job satisfaction and career performance (see Table 3 in the appendix), these relationships become non-significant and marginally significant when personality typology is included in the model (see Table 4 in the appendix). Since extraversion highly relates with all four factors (see Table 4 in the appendix) and multiple session participants tend to be higher in extraversion, the relationship between TMI attendance and job satisfaction and career performance is not clear.

It is interesting to note that on every one of the 34 items loaded on one of the four factors, the percentage of those indicating strongly agree was higher for those having attended three or more programs. To get into the details a bit more, I looked at those items loaded on personal efficacy and have listed those with the highest percentage difference between the two groups and those with the lowest percentage difference (see table below).

To offer an observation, I would suggest that the majority of items with the highest percentage difference are closely aligned with the objectives of TMI programs whereas the items with the lowest percentage difference are not (to my knowledge) stated objectives of TMI's educational mission. Therefore the areas with greatest evidence of long-term benefits are consistent with what would be expected. The 8 items with the highest difference are:

Question	Percentage of MP Respondents indicating Strongly Agree	Percentage of GO Respondents indicating Strongly Agree	Difference
"I have a more expansive vision of how the parts of my life relate to a whole."	61.30	25.29	36.01
"I am more actively involved in my own personal development."	62.45	30.65	31.80
"I take actions that are more true to my sense of self."	45.21	18.77	26.44
"I have a clearer sense of purpose in my life."	46.74	20.31	26.43
"I am less anxious about my future."	44.06	18.77	25.29
"I am more clear about what is important to me."	51.34	27.20	24.14
"I have been able to resolve an important issue or challenge in my life."	32.57	11.88	20.69
"I act on my values more consistently."	34.10	14.18	19.92

The 7 items with the lowest difference are:

Question	Percentage of MP Respondents indicating Strongly Agree	Percentage of GO Respondents indicating Strongly Agree	Difference
"I have a more open communication with my family."	18.01	8.43	9.58
"I am more productive at work."	14.18	4.60	9.58
"I am more able to listen non-defensively to criticism."	21.07	11.11	9.96
"I have a clear sense of further development I need to accomplish."	40.23	29.50	10.73
"I am more successful in my career."	17.97	6.56	11.41
"I have more balance among my work, my family, and my community."	22.61	11.11	11.50
"I have developed new friends."	20.31	8.43	11.88

While those attending multiple programs claim to more strongly agree with the clarity of their sense of purpose and other quality of life dimensions, could it be merely a function of degree of agreement? Maybe those who have only attended the Gateway program are more likely to agree (rather than strongly agree) with these questions relative to those attending multiple programs? In fact it is the other way around; though the difference is small (the average agree response to each of the items under the factors of self-efficacy and life satisfaction was 40.84% of the GO respondents and 42.14% of the MP respondents). It is worth noting that those who have attended multiple programs are more likely than those who have only attended Gateway to both agree and strongly agree with the following items:

1. "I am a more effective decision maker."
2. "I surface issues that others are reluctant to talk about."
3. "I have a clear sense of further development I need to accomplish."
4. "I have more balance among my work, my family, and my community."
5. "I am more able to listen non-defensively to criticism."
6. "I am more successful in my career."
7. "I have deepened my relationship with existing friends."
8. "I have a more open communication with my family."
9. "I am more productive at work."
10. "I have developed new friends."
11. "I have been able to resolve an important issue or challenge in my life."
12. "I am more confident in my interaction with others."

For the 12 items loaded on life satisfaction, job satisfaction, and career performance, the differences are not as dramatic between the two groups but the same trend exists. The 5 items with the highest difference are:

Question	Percentage of MP Respondents indicating Strongly Agree	Percentage of GO Respondents indicating Strongly Agree	Difference
"So far I have gotten the important things in my life."	34.48	20.31	14.17

Question	Percentage of MP Respondents indicating Strongly Agree	Percentage of GO Respondents indicating Strongly Agree	Difference
"The conditions of my life are excellent."	33.72	20.69	13.03
"I am satisfied with my life."	32.18	19.54	12.64
"I like my job better than the average worker does."	36.76	25.79	10.97
"I find real enjoyment in my work."	30.31	20.40	9.91

The 4 items with the lowest difference are:

Question	Percentage of MP Respondents indicating Strongly Agree	Percentage of GO Respondents indicating Strongly Agree	Difference
"At work I am viewed by my supervisor as an exceptional performer."	29.84	25.00	4.84
"I feel that my career is progressing very well compared with my peers."	20.00	14.46	5.54
"Most days I am enthusiastic about my work."	23.92	15.75	8.17
"The people I work with would say that I am very successful."	30.68	22.27	8.41

Across all 12 items the MP group averaged a higher percentage of agree responses than those from the Gateway group. Again, the difference is small. On average 40.89% of GO respondents agreed with these 12 items in comparison to 41.38% of MP respondents. Those who have attended multiple programs are more likely than those who have only attended Gateway to both agree and strongly agree with the following questions:

1. "The conditions of my life are excellent."
2. "At work, I am viewed by my supervisor as an exceptional performer."
3. "Most days I am enthusiastic about my work."
4. "Compared to other people my age and who are involved in the same occupation or types of work I do, I feel that I am very successful."
5. "The people I work with would say that I am very successful."
6. "I find real enjoyment in my work."
7. "I feel that my career is progressing very well compared with my peers."
8. "In most ways my life is close to ideal."

Section 4 – Qualitative Analysis and Conclusions

In addition to scaled items, survey respondents were given the opportunity to address four open-ended items:

- List three to five important events in your life, positive or negative, after your first program at TMI.
- How would you describe TMI to someone who may be interested in attending for the first time?
- How would you describe the kind of person who would get the most out of attending the Gateway Voyage program?
- What is most memorable in your experience at TMI?

In the interest of addressing the question of effects from long-term participation in TMI programs, I have chosen to focus my analysis on the last item. To do that I created four categories of comments to organize the different kinds of responses:

- Mystical Experience – reference to experiences of meta-normal functioning
- Personal Learning and Development – reference to lessons learned, insights generated, personal growth/healing
- Belonging – reference to the value of or connection to others in the program
- Gestalt – reference to the intangibles or indivisibility of the unique features of TMI

There were no restrictions in assignment of comments to categories, and therefore, individual responses could be represented in all four. The fact that a majority of comments were represented in more that one category is indicative of the length of responses.

Category	GO	MP
Mystical Experience	107	135
Personal Learning & Development	126	116
Belonging	100	96
Gestalt	108	62

Sample of Respondent Comments by Category (in some cases these are merely excerpts)

1. Mystical Experience

GO:

- Finding there was a ghost in my room (seriously!)
- Meeting with a guide of mine
- Hearing the ground drink the rain that fell
- Being shown an image of my Higher Self by my deceased mother

- Seeing huge statues carved out of milk, with fine detail, floating in one area of far space and knowing they were The Dreamers.
- Contact with deceased parents and others
- Awakening a past life
- Having an implant removed by these beings I would never have imagined – and afterwards being pain-free for the first time in a long time
- The walk in the outdoors with trees, stones, animals, etc. "talking" to me
- Remembering how I went to/was the stars as I fell asleep as a child
- Connecting to other participant and facilitators through telepathy

MP:

- A non-physical meeting with my family. Very healing.
- Meeting my grandmother for the first time and realizing that she is available to help me.
- In the closing circle we "fell" into a spontaneous silent meditation and atmospheric Presence moved into the room that was sooooo powerful, tangible, and loving... no one said a word or stirred for over two hours.
- The sudden, acute awareness of off-planet entities communicating directly to me which has caused an irreversible (I wouldn't want it reversed) personal paradigm shift in my consciousness in how to approach life
- I had an interaction with my son who passed away at birth as a result of an auto accident. It was a beautiful, playful and deeply emotional experience all at the same time.
- The most meaningful in an on-going way is my discovery of inner guides who regularly provide me with direction for both my inner and outer life.

- Being visited by Mother Mary, who presented me with a long-stemmed black rose and murmured, "I embrace my shadow, for it illuminates my light" (this was seminal, in that it taught me that I need not get rid of anything).
- Visiting the "city of light"
- When I found a piece of myself I didn't even know was separate from me and desperately trying to get my attention and "come home."
- Being with Spirit/all that is/the divine oneness totally and in the state of bliss
- Having a vision of the woman I would eventually live with 8 years later

2. Personal Learning and Development

GO:

- I am so pleased to understand at a deep level that "we are more than our physical bodies." I am no longer afraid of death and feel more connected to the universe and my fellow creatures and nature.
- When I experienced my energy body as fluid nature. I have had continuous muscular skeletal pain for years. I was able to move the energy body in such a way I felt my physical body release, relax and heal from the inside out.
- I was able to accept my limitations and inner barriers and judgments, and forgive myself for it
- The experience of peace in focus 21
- Feeling myself being able to relax and quiet my mind
- I felt the most relaxed and soft and open I have ever felt
- I connected right after the video showing the pics of universe being sooo small... at that point my reality was shaken to such a level that I literally collapsed on the grounds and cried for several minutes. My concepts of God and my placement within the Universe were reconstructed that day.

- A meeting having cried with oneself of the young time together.
- Learning to trust myself and to know myself better
- How we elevate each others consciousness
- Realizing how dumb I've been
- My ability to "see" my thinking and "feel" higher intelligence. Feeling of peace and clarity.
- Being more open to changes in your life and life experience expectancies
- The first time I was actually aware of being OPEN to the messages that were there for me to hear.
- The realization of another frontier of exploration
- The skills I learned to allow me to continue exploration within myself which have made me a better a person.
- What I remember most about TMI is awaking to the concept that we, the human race, strongly affect each other with our energy, and that we are responsible for our own energy, as well as responsible for deflecting the energy of others when it is meant to harm.
- The realization that life must be lived in balance and harmony between the spiritual and physical worlds
- Discovering the clown chakra
- Realizing I am still alive

MP:

- Understood at a cellular level how time is just a construct of our physical dimension
- My increased awareness of the omens in everyday life
- The feeling, presence of knowing that I am loved and have much great support
- Mostly it was the healings and personal lessons learned about myself that were so unexpected, but were so profound. I am a very different person, much more whole than before.
- The day that I found out that my life is nothing more than what I say it is, whatever beliefs I adopt is how life appears to

me. And that physically as I had understood it is an illusion. I wasn't what I thought I was. Absolutely mind blowing!! I loved it and I am grateful everyday.

- TMI helped me heal when I was VERY bruised. I will always be grateful.
- Remembrance/Realization that I/we are all already in F27 and beyond, and that C1 is the extension, and that I/we have always been operating multi-dimensionally whether this C1 personality was aware of it or not.
- Finding my inner child and having confidence in myself to dance with others.
- One part of our purpose here on Earth, or one way to look at it, is to enable God to experience the physical. In my case, hear and enjoy music.
- I come back feeling very refreshed and focused
- The subtle changes in me that always follow later
- Discovering how much of my life actually occurs in my head
- I became more fully aware of how fear-based I have lived my life. I realized that I often failed to follow my guidance if I was afraid of possible consequences.
- How I learned to love and trust my self
- Letting go of shame
- The release of many unconscious fears
- Rediscovering how love unites all of us

3. Belonging

   GO:

   - Meeting others with similar goals and desires
   - The wonderful camaraderie with the other participants
   - The People. It was like being back with family, having comfort and feeling secure in my thoughts.
   - The people, the caring and understanding people

- The reaction of all the others when I told my "story". Very supportive!
- Being part of a group where there is so much acceptance and caring and to be able to express a shared belief and not be judged, lectured, scolded or preached to.
- The feeling of knowing everyone, as if I had been there before
- Total group acceptance. No judgments.
- 23 people from all over the world came together as strangers and left as friends
- The camaraderie of the participants. At first, everyone is nervous about opening up, but then amazing things start to happen and everyone becomes very close and supportive
- The energy and environment produced by a group of like minded individuals looking to discover themselves

MP:

- The most memorable thing is the friendship and interactions with the participants
- Being in the incredible energy with the best people in the world
- The other people in the program. I felt totally accepted and loved.
- Discovering the existence of the kinds of people who attend and teach at the institute
- Friendships and shared experiences
- In EVERY class attended, the BONDING within the participants
- Meeting old friends
- Intimate sharing of thoughts that you can only share at TMI
- Shared experiences validating the "realness" of experiences; the precious personal qualities of participants
- Meeting so many other people from all over the world that are open to discuss and share their experiences with you and not be critical of your experiences when you choose to share.
- Meeting wonderful people and feeling them to be a spiritual family

4. Gestalt

GO:

- Everything, everything...
- The whole experience was a paradigm shift for me.
- Ah where to begin. I am very pragmatic and practical... and the psychic tranquility and aura of twinkling creativity pervaded the environment.
- All of it!
- The feeling of coming home. All I have to do is remember that way the buildings looked, or how hot it was that week, or the people I met; I relive the experience every time I think of it. I love that place.
- When I remember the course what fills my mind is the sea, the moon, the trees, and the view over the surrounding area.
- Waking up to "cable car" and bouncing out of bed eager to see what we'll be doing for the day!
- Freedom from the outside world, no clocks, TV, newspaper. Time to get in touch with your inner spirit.
- My experience there is a soft, mellow collage of great energy.
- Going for a walk and having butterflies dance all around me
- Listening to Joe McMoneagle
- Waking up one morning and seeing 4 deer standing on their hind legs, arranged in a circle in the mist
- The gentleness of the process
- All the laughter

MP:

- The complete peace the minute your step onto the grounds
- MOST memorable. Just one. That's impossible! How do you choose among dying and learning the meaning of life; learning about love in the deepest possible way; finding yourself;

truly understanding the nature of reality; transforming your life and health and relationships? I can't! Each time is as amazing as the last.

- It is not one event but the collective whole that brings my smile
- Hauntingly memorable
- TMI is like a hospital for the soul
- There is so much... Laughter!!! Space and time to contemplate. Beautiful nature. Compassionate and extraordinary companions. Heart opening – both in a sort of general sense of feeling of love for the other participants, but also in a physical sense – that feeling you get in the chest like you might explode. This force of "loosh" that is almost too much for the physical body to handle. Becoming aware of guides or non-physical friends who are looking out for you, and being overwhelmed by their loosh, knowing you are never alone.
- There is no one memorable experience. The whole program is the memorable experience.
- All the programs that I have attended are the most memorable and fascinating week that I have ever experienced. I love TMI and am looking forward to going there again, again, and again...
- The whole place tends to be a Wonderland.
- The tapes, and the way one experiences them, i.e., the booth itself
- I felt like I experienced a sense of home for the first time in my life (I had a decent childhood with a definite sense of love in the family).
- I drove to TMI the first time and Robert Monroe followed me home in a blue Pinto to give directions and guidance.
- The sense of peace and serenity
- These are the things of Monroe, a tool for a beleaguered humanity to accelerate the journey home

I provided a lengthy sampling in order to demonstrate the rich variety of personalities evoked by the individual responses. It is also interesting to note how evenly distributed the responses were within the four categories and among their respective groups. While there are many shared and common themes here, in the end a distinct qualitative difference exists between the GO and the MP respondents. To understand this difference it is important to illustrate the notion of an evolutionary arrow within the dynamic forces of life itself. Growth is a process of change that results from successful adaptation to one's environment. The resulting change is often limited to an assimilation of new information within an existing state of mental functioning – horizontal development. When a more radical response is required to accommodate new frames of reference, self-transcendence will result if a person is successful in making the adjustment – vertical development. In essence, the new sense of self emerges from its embeddedness within an existing state of mental functioning. This emergence is a result of acquiring a new orientation that includes a degree of objectivity about oneself and others that is inclusive of subjective experience (what was present with no conscious awareness).

It is relevant to note that both groups of respondents in this survey have had monumental shifts in how they perceive themselves and the world around them. However, if I were to try to describe the difference I observed between the GO and MP respondents, I would use words like depth of self-awareness, greater personal disclosure, range of metaphors or references for sharing their experiences, degree of experience with inner exploration, and appreciation for the gifts they have received. In the Personal Learning & Development category, the MP respondents related to personal healing, overcoming fears, trust in a higher self, and the experience of being loved to a much higher degree than the GO respondents. The point is the degree in which the words they used expressed something more integrated into a sense of themselves (more affective in nature rather than merely abstract). What does this mean? Based on the statistical analysis, the answer to the question of how the MP respondents can be so "high on life" (while at the same time be at odds "with the way things are") seems to imply a state of ego development indicative of an ability to recognize the limitations to any perspective. To take this a step further, MP respondents more willingly engage others for the challenge it poses to their worldview as the means for growing more expansive in their experiences (i.e., to intentionally seek means to grow beyond where they are rather than merely having it happen as a function of circumstances they encounter).

While there is evidence to suggest that MP participants have made major shifts in consciousness, specific characteristics of individuals from this group yet need to be identified and sorted via a process of comparative analysis. Further to this point are the relatively poor observational skills of extraverted/introverted intuitive types, which characterize the vast majority of participants in the MP group. Individuals who have an introverted intuitive or extroverted intuitive personality type can pay such little attention to details at times that their credibility regarding the facts of a specific experience is suspect. The next phase of this study will look more closely at a representative set of the MP group to further evaluate the effects of long-term participation in TMI programs.

Appendix

Table 1

Priorities and Direction of Functions in Each Type

ISTJ	ISFJ	INFJ	INTJ
Dominant S (I)	Dominant S (I)	Dominant N (I)	Dominant N (I)
Auxiliary T (E)	Auxiliary F (E)	Auxiliary F (E)	Auxiliary T (E)
ISTP	**ISFP**	**INFP**	**INTP**
Dominant T (I)	Dominant F (I)	Dominant F (I)	Dominant T (I)
Auxiliary S (E)	Auxiliary S (E)	Auxiliary N (E)	Auxiliary N (E)
ESTP	**ESFP**	**ENFP**	**ENTP**
Dominant S (E)	Dominant S (E)	Dominant N (E)	Dominant N (E)
Auxiliary T (I)	Auxiliary F (I)	Auxiliary F (I)	Auxiliary T (I)
ESTJ	**ESFJ**	**ENFJ**	**ENTJ**
Dominant T (E)	Dominant F (E)	Dominant F (E)	Dominant T (E)
Auxiliary S (I)	Auxiliary S (I)	Auxiliary N (I)	Auxiliary N (I)

Table 2

Means, Standard Deviations, and Correlations
Note: Correlations with absolute values greater than 0.13, 0.10, 0.074, and 0.068 are significant at p < .001, p < 0.01, p< 0.05, and p < 0.10 levels respectively

Variables	N	Mean	Std Dev	1	2	3	4	5	6	7	8	9
1 TMI Attendance	694	2.48	1.50	-								
2 Efficacy	613	3.86	0.64	0.36	-							
3 Life Satisfaction	633	3.75	0.88	0.19	0.45	-						
4 Job Satisfaction	622	3.77	0.93	0.11	0.35	0.61	-					
5 Career Performance	591	3.76	0.77	0.16	0.41	0.53	0.62	-				
6 Age	690	6.75	2.02	0.14	0.05	0.17	0.19	0.08	-			
7 Education	694	5.11	1.46	0.13	0.02	0.11	0.13	0.08	0.15	-		
8 Income	622	3.42	1.86	0.12	0.01	0.11	0.05	0.26	0.04	0.21	-	
9 Extraversion (K-B Type)	587	5.48	2.40	0.07	0.22	0.21	0.27	0.24	0.14	-0.04	0.04	
10 Sensing (K-B Type)	587	6.24	3.68	-0.02	-0.13	-0.06	-0.08	-0.03	-0.03	-0.01	0.16	-0.1
11 Thinking (K-B Type)	587	8.15	3.90	-0.03	-0.21	-0.13	-0.16	-0.10	-0.04	-0.02	0.08	-0.1
12 Judging (K-B Type)	587	11.12	4.25	-0.02	-0.12	-0.09	-0.12	-0.07	0.00	0.05	0.09	-0.2
13 Age Squared	690	49.64	25.27	0.13	0.06	0.18	0.19	0.09	0.98	0.15	0.00	0.1
14 Single	694	0.18	0.38	-0.05	-0.08	-0.19	-0.12	-0.13	-0.40	-0.08	-0.15	-0.
15 Married	694	0.51	0.50	0.03	0.06	0.21	0.07	0.18	0.08	0.06	0.09	-0.0
16 Divorced	694	0.22	0.41	0.00	-0.04	-0.12	-0.05	-0.10	0.16	-0.02	0.03	0.
17 Widowed	694	0.05	0.21	0.06	0.04	0.10	0.09	0.06	0.19	0.01	-0.03	0.
18 Gender (Male)	694	0.51	0.50	0.03	-0.03	-0.06	-0.16	-0.06	-0.12	0.02	0.25	-0.
19 Unemployed	694	0.05	0.22	-0.16	-0.03	-0.11	-0.14	-0.24	-0.16	-0.11	-0.20	-0.1
20 Retired	694	0.15	0.36	0.09	0.04	0.13	0.01	-0.01	0.39	0.03	-0.10	0.
21 White	694	0.86	0.35	0.05	-0.01	0.09	0.07	0.07	0.10	0.07	0.07	-0.
22 Indian	694	0.01	0.08	0.04	0.04	0.02	-0.03	-0.04	-0.05	-0.08	-0.04	0.
23 Black	694	0.02	0.14	-0.05	-0.06	-0.04	-0.05	-0.02	-0.10	0.04	-0.06	0.
24 Hispanic	694	0.03	0.18	-0.08	0.05	-0.06	-0.04	0.01	-0.02	-0.04	0.01	0.
25 Asian	694	0.03	0.17	-0.02	0.01	-0.05	-0.05	-0.09	-0.05	0.00	-0.03	0.
26 Other Race	694	0.03	0.18	0.01	0.00	0.00	0.01	-0.03	-0.03	-0.07	-0.04	-0.
27 Partner Income	606	0.86	1.37	-0.03	0.08	0.17	0.10	0.04	-0.05	-0.05	-0.31	0.

10	11	12	13	14	15	16	17	18	19	20	21	22	23	24	25	26
-																
0.46	-															
0.57	0.43	-														
-0.02	-0.03	0.00	-													
-0.02	0.04	-0.06	-0.36	-												
0.06	0.02	0.10	0.05	-0.47	-											
-0.02	-0.04	-0.02	0.15	-0.25	-0.54	-										
-0.01	-0.02	-0.05	0.22	-0.10	-0.23	-0.12	-									
0.12	0.24	0.03	-0.11	0.07	0.05	-0.09	-0.12	-								
-0.02	0.01	0.00	-0.15	0.11	-0.02	-0.03	-0.05	-0.03	-							
0.09	0.10	0.04	0.43	-0.13	0.05	-0.01	0.13	-0.04	-0.10	-						
-0.06	-0.02	-0.01	0.10	-0.04	-0.01	0.04	0.09	-0.05	-0.02	0.03	-					
0.01	-0.02	0.04	-0.03	0.01	0.04	-0.04	-0.02	0.07	-0.02	0.02	-0.19	-				
0.07	0.05	0.09	-0.09	0.13	-0.03	-0.05	-0.03	0.01	-0.03	-0.03	-0.34	-0.01	-			
0.02	0.05	-0.03	-0.02	-0.03	0.01	-0.02	-0.04	-0.02	-0.01	-0.04	-0.47	-0.01	-0.03	-		
0.04	-0.05	-0.02	-0.07	0.01	-0.01	0.05	-0.04	0.00	0.11	-0.03	-0.44	-0.01	-0.02	-0.03	-	
-0.03	-0.01	-0.02	-0.03	0.00	0.05	-0.04	-0.04	0.07	-0.01	0.04	-0.46	-0.01	-0.03	-0.04	-0.03	-
-0.07	-0.16	-0.05	-0.06	-0.17	0.42	-0.29	-0.07	-0.17	0.11	0.00	0.03	0.07	-0.03	-0.04	0.04	-0.03

Table 3

Multivariate Regression Results Excluding Personality Variables

Dependent Variables	Personal Efficacy	Life Satisfaction	Job Satisfaction	Career Performance
Independent Variables				
TMI Attendance	0.135***	0.094***	0.056*	0.053*
Age	-0.075	-0.129	-0.080	-0.242**
Age Squared	0.006	0.013	0.012	0.021**
Education	0.007	0.012	0.043	-0.005
Income	0.002	0.076**	0.037	0.117***
Single	-0.357**	-0.157	-0.402†	0.002
Married	-0.199	0.218	-0.284	0.210
Divorced	-0.283*	-0.106	-0.478*	-0.068
Widowed	-0.070	0.464	-0.017	0.180
Gender (male)	-0.114*	-0.159†	-0.258**	-0.241***
Unemployed	0.167	-0.054	-0.310†	-0.510***
Retired	0.039	0.237†	-0.212	-0.138
Race (white)	-0.100	0.081	0.072	-0.017
Partner Income	0.047*	0.121***	0.086*	0.042
R2	0.16	0.18	0.12	0.18
F	6.06***	7.07***	4.34***	7.06***
Df	14, 448	14, 448	14, 448	14, 448
† p < 0.10 * p < 0.05 ** p < 0.01 ***p < 0.001				

Table 4

Multivariate Regression Results Including Personality Variables

Dependent Variables	Personal Efficacy	Life Satisfaction	Job Satisfaction	Career Performance
Independent Variables				
TMI Attendance	0.121***	0.081**	0.036	0.044†
Age	-0.048	-0.121	-0.124	-0.261**
Age Squared	0.003	0.012	0.015	0.023**
Education	0.022	0.026	0.061*	0.001
Income	-0.010	0.054*	0.007	0.101***
Extraversion (K-B Type)	0.044***	0.053**	0.079***	0.061***
Sensing (K-B Type)	-0.008	0.008	0.014	0.006
Thinking (K-B Type)	-0.021*	-0.023†	-0.011	-0.013
Judging (K-B Type)	-0.001	-0.007	-0.017	-0.007
Single	-0.370**	-0.233	-0.385 †	0.051
Married	-0.199	0.160	-0.240	0.268
Divorced	-0.277*	-0.209	-0.437*	-0.029
Widowed	-0.058	0.393	0.013	0.229
Gender (male)	-0.048	-0.121	-0.224*	-0.187*
Unemployed	0.208†	0.031	-0.368 †	-0.548***
Retired	0.068	0.233	-0.248	-0.146
Race (white)	-0.075	0.116	0.096	0.003
Partner Income	0.022	0.085*	0.055	0.024
R2	0.20	0.20	0.17	0.22
F	5.56***	5.44***	4.44***	6.42
Df	18, 398	18. 398	18, 398	18, 398
† p < 0.10 * p < 0.05 ** p < 0.01 ***p < 0.001				

Attachment 2

Phase II Research Protocol on the Effects of Long-Term Participation in The Monroe Institute Programs

THE INITIAL GOAL was to identify a representative group from those who had participated in the first phase of the study. While I was limited to those who had indicated a willingness to participate in a follow-up interview, that number exceeded 200 of the individuals in the Multiple Programs (MP) group. From this subset I sorted based on the following demographic dimensions:

- Gender
- Age
- Civil Status
- Household Income
- Education

A group of 35 was identified and a letter of invitation prepared and distributed under the signature of the president of the Monroe Institute, Skip Atwater, explaining the purpose of the study and introducing me as the principal investigator. I then sent a more detailed outline of the specific steps in the interview process including the following list of questions I referenced as the interview guide:

1. Where did you grow up? List the various locations and dates, as appropriate.

2. Who were the most important members of your family to you (including your extended family)? Describe them and frequency of contact.

3. What were some of your favorite memories of family life? Least favorite memories?

4. What did school mean for you – how did it affect your life? What did you enjoy the most about school (both through high school and after high school)? What did you not enjoy about school (both through high school and after high school)?

5. What would you describe as the most important experiences in your life before you left home and began to live on your own?

6. Who have been the most influential people in your life after you left home? Why?

7. In the early stage of your working life, how would you answer someone if they asked you: "What do you do?" How would you answer that question in a latter or current stage?

8. What jobs have you held? What was the most rewarding aspect of your work?

9. What amount of time have you spent living alone and/or with someone else in an intimate relationship? How important is it to you to have a life partner? If appropriate, what is the most significant thing you have learned about yourself and others as a result of having a life partner?

10. How many people do you count among your friends? How would you describe them (qualities, characteristics, why you count them among your friends)?

11. What events or ongoing activities have been or continue to be instrumental to your growth and development?

12. How would you describe your perfect day?

Those who were interested emailed me with a phone number and I made contact to schedule an interview. This accounted for the initial 8 interviews conducted over the first 3 months of the study. While I did get 5 individuals declining to participate, far more simply did not respond either due to changes in their email address or uncertainty about the time commitment. Consequently, I spent several months in follow-up mode securing another 9 interviews. The result was a nine-month process for completing the 17 interviews. To the degree possible, I sought to do each interview in person and was successful in 8 out of the 17. On average, each interview lasted 3 hours even though I had asked for only 90 minutes.

At the conclusion of each interview, I asked for a commitment to participate in a multi-rater assessment using an online psychometric instrument (the description of the instrument was included in my initial letter to everyone). The objective was to understand how others familiar with the participants in the study had observed them on a set of dimensions indicative of their interpersonal effectiveness. Two individuals declined due to personal reasons. Of the 15 who agreed, 14 completed the process which added another two months on average for each participant since they were now responsible not only for completing the survey themselves but for identifying others who knew them well enough to also complete the online survey. In the end, data collection, comprised of 17 interviews (52 hours of tape recorded conversations and 300 hundred pages of notes) and 14 multi-rater assessments (210 pages of summary results), took one year to complete.

Attachment 3

Demographic Profile
of the Participants

The participants in this study were a mix of Caucasian men and women post mid-life. There were seven men and ten women. At the time the interviews were conducted, their ages ranged from 44 to 72. Average and mean age for the group was 57. The average age among the men was 56 and among the women 58. The civil status of the group included eight who were married (including three who had been married previously), five who were divorced, and four who had never been married. Along gender lines, five men & three women were married, two men & three women were divorced, and four women had never been married.

Total household income varied widely from less than $49,999 to more than $300,000 as the following table illustrates:

Total household income	Men	Women
$30,000-$49,999		1
$50,000-$69,999		3
$70,000-$99,999	2	3*
$100,000-$149,999	3*	1*
$150,000-$199,999	2*	1
$300,000+		1*

Illustrated with an * are income categories populated by the individuals who were married. As to be expected, the married participants in this study averaged higher total household income. Among the men, those with more than $100,000 were married. Among the women, however, it was more widely dispersed with one over $300,000, one between $100,000 and $149,999, and one between $70,000 and $99,999.

Education levels also varied widely across the group from some college to post-doctoral:

Education	Men	Women
Some College	2	1
College Degree	3	3
Master's/Professional Degree (MBA, Medical, etc.)	2	3
PhD		2
Post-Doctoral (M.D.)		1

As illustrated, the women in the group were the most educated on a formal basis. Income levels among the women were higher for those with the more advanced education levels and it is worth noting that civil status only moderately impacted their reported income levels. Among those in the top three education levels, two were divorced, one had never been married, and another had only recently married and household income did not reflect her spouse. Among the men, those who were married reported the top five incomes. Across both genders, those with the lowest reported household incomes were single.

Attachment 4

Other Personal Development Activities by Participant

Audrey	Attended Esalen (multiple week-long sessions) and a Barbara Brennen sponsored workshop, and has taken several road trips during periods of major changes in her personal and professional life (each lasting from one to three months).
Beatrice	Has taken voice lessons, attended Byron Katie and Barbara Brennen sponsored workshops, and took a three-month road trip during a period of change in her personal and professional life spending time in an ashram and at the Light Center in North Carolina learning to meditate.
Carl	Has been doing Transcendental Meditation for many years.
Deborah	Has been doing Abraham work with Jerry and Esther Hicks for a number of years and also has done Orin and DaBen work with Sanaya Roman and Duane Packer, respectively.
Elaine	Trained as a singer and continues to do breathing exercises everyday. Completed training in Reiki.
Frank	Undertook intensive yoga training in early adulthood, has done past life regression analysis, read the works of Elizabeth Kubler-Ross on death and dying (became a hospice volunteer), and did research on Hindu philosophy.
Gwen	Has done critical reading of the works of Mary Summer Rain, Carolyn Myss, and The Tibetan Book of Living and Dying; more recently worked with Gangaji (Toni Roberson).
Helen	Has worked with Barry Neil Kaufman (Founder of the Options Institute), underwent personal therapy, completed studies in accelerated learning.

Isaac	Has done significant astrological work (studied to become an astrologer), became an accomplished hypnotist, and continues to attend meetings of the Religious Society of Friends (Quakers).
Julie	Attended personal transformation workshops of various kinds.
Kenneth	Studied religion and philosophy in college, after college began reading Edgar Cayce's work and attended workshops at the Associate for Research and Enlightenment (A.R.E.), and began a regular meditation practice.
Lyle	Read widely in occult literature, began a regular meditation practice in mid-life, has been involved in numerous creative activities since childhood such as drawing, music, and filmmaking.
Margaret	Has done transactional analysis work, read the works of Jane Roberts (Seth), began to read more widely in occult philosophy in mid-life, and completed training in Reiki.
Norris	Was a member of the Rosicrucians for many years, read widely in occult philosophy, has certifications from HearthMath, Music for Healing, and NLP (Neuro-linguistic Programming), and is a certified leadership coach.
Olivia	After completing her MBA, became a certified massage therapist. Throughout her life has read widely in occult philosophy and completed The Course in Miracles.
Peter	Has read widely in religion and occult philosophy.
Regina	Developed a wide repertoire of physical skills in things like skiing, canoeing, rowing, and dance. Studied qigong under Chow Ming. Became a Feldenkrais practitioner.

Attachment 5

Example of Multiple Intelligences by Participant

	Music/ Dance/Art/ Film Production	Creation and Operation of Independently Owned Business	Writing/ Computer Programming	Acting/ Public Speaking/ Teaching	Athletics/ Outdoor Activities
Audrey		Started and currently runs an executive and life coaching practice.	Author of multiple books.	Teaching and public speaking as a consultant and executive coach.	Extreme white water rafting & kayaking.
Beatrice	Song writer and singer. Performs publicly.		Book author, technical writer for a software company.		Sailing as a child.
Carl		Runs several businesses of his own that include farming and energy distribution.	Book co-author.		Canoeing, Rowing, and Baseball as a child. Became a Life Guard. Continues to play slow pitch softball.
Deborah	Self-trained painter.	Currently runs her own business as a physician.		Teaching part-time at the University level.	Biking and yoga.
Elaine	Opera Singer – performed at the MET in New York – and songwriter in her early career.	Started and currently runs a management consulting practice with her partner.	Author of short stories, poetry, and scholarly articles and books.	Teaching and public speaking as a consultant in the field of organization development.	Softball, basketball, track and field, and field hockey in school. Currently a stable of horses.

	Music/ Dance/Art/ Film Production	Creation and Operation of Independently Owned Business	Writing/ Computer Programming	Acting/ Public Speaking/ Teaching	Athletics/ Outdoor Activities
Frank		Started a manufacturing business and sold it. Currently runs his second business in manufacturing supply.		Studied acting in Paris after college.	Cooking, car repair, and general mechanics. Outward bound, cross-country running, and wrestling in school. Yoga as a young adult. Currently rides motorcycles, pilot's sailboats, and has gone skydiving.
Gwen		Started and currently runs a hypnotherapy practice.	Book author.		
Helen	Plays the violin and guitar. Uses music in her education and therapeutic practice.	Formed and currently runs a therapeutic practice for children with feeding, swallowing, oral-motor, and pre-speech problems.	Author of scholarly articles/books.	Teaching and public speaking in continuing education programs.	Camping, hiking, climbing trees as a child. Rowing and hiking yet today.
Isaac		Started and currently runs a translation business.	Astrological writing. Scholarly articles in transpersonal psychology.	Shakes-pearean trained actor. Taught English in Saudi Arabia. Former principal of a school in Australia.	Yoga

	Music/ Dance/Art/ Film Production	Creation and Operation of Independently Owned Business	Writing/ Computer Programming	Acting/ Public Speaking/ Teaching	Athletics/ Outdoor Activities
Julie		Started and ran IT consulting business.	Technical writer for various organizations and clients.		Cheer-leading in high school.
Kenneth	Professio-nally trained guitarist.		Technical writer and software programmer.	Part-time music teacher.	Surfing as a young adult.
Lyle	Plays guitar, trained in music theory. Artist in the field of animation and film production (created a way to make 3D animation before the era of computers).	Started and ran IT consulting business.	Software programmer.		Yoga
Margaret	Drawing and illustration (works part-time as an illustrator for a museum of natural history).	Started and currently runs a horse training business.		Mentoring emotionally disturbed children.	4-H in high school. Professio-nally trained horse trainer with horses of her own.
Norris	Musician certified in the Music for Healing and Transition Program.	Independent consultant in the field of technical project management.		Hospice volunteer. Certified professional coach.	Camping, hiking (was a boy scout). Private pilot license to fly small aircraft.

	Music/ Dance/Art/ Film Production	Creation and Operation of Independently Owned Business	Writing/ Computer Programming	Acting/ Public Speaking/ Teaching	Athletics/ Outdoor Activities
Olivia	Ballet and modern dance.	Founded and sold a computer supplies company. Founded and currently runs a business in health and wellness offering massage, exercise and diet classes, and meditation. Founded and currently runs a staffing/ employment services business.			Gifted athlete. Performed in a number of fields including skating, swimming, sailing, gymnastics, and track and field. Became a lifeguard as a teenager.
Peter				Studied acting in an after school theater program for 6 years. Went to college on a theater scholarship.	ROTC in high school. Biking, camping, and hiking.
Regina	Profes- sionally trained dancer.	Started and currently runs a physical therapy practice. Previously made her living as an author.	Writer of plays, short stories, and articles for magazines.	Spent her early career as a teacher (K-12). Also taught canoeing and rowing. Did further qualifications in theater and drama.	Canoeing, rowing, yoga. Feldenkrais practitioner.

Attachment 6

The Leadership Circle Profile Dimensions and Definitions

THE CREATIVE LEADERSHIP competencies measure key behaviors and internal assumptions that lead to high fulfillment and achievement. The Relating dimension measures one's capability to relate to others in a way that brings out the best in people, groups and organizations. It comprises the following competencies:

- *Caring Connection* measures interest in and ability to form warm, caring relationships.
- *Foster Team Play* measures ability to foster high-performance teamwork among team members.
- *Collaborator* measures the extent of engagement with others in a manner that allows the parties involved to discover common ground, find mutually beneficial agreements, and create productive working relationships.
- *Mentoring and Developing* measures ability to facilitate the development others through growth-enhancing relationships.
- *Interpersonal Intelligence* measures quality of listening and engagement, dealing with the feelings of others, and management of one's own feelings in conflict and controversy.

The Self-Awareness dimension measures one's orientation to ongoing professional and personal development, as well as the degree to which inner self-awareness through high integrity leadership. It comprises the following competencies:

- *Selfless Leader* measures the extent which one pursues service over self-interest. It measures a very high state of personal awareness where the need for credit and personal ambition is far less important than creating results which serve a common good.

- *Balance* measures ability to keep a healthy balance between business and family, activity and reflection, work and leisure, etc., in the midst of the conflicting tensions of modern life.
- *Composure* measures ability to remain composed and centered with a balanced and focused perspective while in the midst of high-tension situations.
- *Personal Learner* measures the degree to which one demonstrates a strong and active interest in learning, personal, and professional growth.

The Authenticity dimension measures one's capability to relate to others in an authentic, courageous, and high integrity manner. It comprises the following competencies:

- *Integrity* measures consistency of adherence to the set of values and principles one espouses.
- *Courageous Authenticity* measures willingness to take tough stands, bring up risky topics or issues others avoid discussing, and openly deals with difficult relationship problems or issues.

The Systems Awareness dimension measures the degree to which awareness is focused on whole system improvement and community welfare, i.e., the integral relationship between long-term community welfare and individual interests. It comprises the following competencies:

- *Community Concern* measures the extent to which one links their legacy to service of community and global welfare.
- *Sustainable Productivity* measures ability to achieve results in a way that maintains or enhances the overall long-term effectiveness of the organization or collective enterprise.
- *Systems Thinking* measures the degree of thinking and acting from a whole system perspective as well as the extent of decision making in light of the long-term health of the whole.

The Achieving dimension measures the extent to which one offers visionary, authentic, and high achievement leadership. It comprises the following competencies:

- *Strategic Focus* measures the extent of strategic thinking.
- *Purposeful and Visionary* measures the extent of clear communication and commitment to personal purpose and vision.
- *Achieves Results* measures the degree of goal directedness, goal achievement, and high performance.
- *Decisiveness* measures degree of comfort moving forward in uncertainty and an ability to make decisions under pressure.

The reactive leadership styles reflect inner beliefs that limit building effective relationships, encouraging authentic expression, and achieving results in the common good. The Controlling dimension measures the extent to which one establishes a sense of personal worth through task accomplishment and personal achievement. It comprises the following tendencies:

- *Perfect* measures the need to attain flawless results and perform to extremely high standards in order to feel secure and worthwhile as a person.
- *Driven* measures the consistency of operating in overdrive or beyond the boundaries of a well-balanced orientation.
- *Ambition* measures the need to get ahead, acquire more power & influence, and be seen as better than others.
- *Autocratic* measures consistency of acting forcefully and aggressively with a goal of being in control.

The Protecting dimension measures the degree in which one remains distant, aloof, hidden, cynical, righteous or superior in order to avoid situations with a perceived risk of exposure and vulnerability. It comprises the following tendencies:

- *Arrogance* measures the tendency to project a "better than thou" attitude – behavior that is experienced as superior, egotistical, and self-centered.
- *Critical* measures consistency of undermining the ideas and thoughts of others through non-empathetic questioning and comments.

- *Distance* measures degree in which a sense of personal worth and security is established through withdrawal either by an attitude of aloofness or a sense of superiority.

The Complying dimension measures the degree of self-denial to avoid upsetting others by not meeting their perceived expectations. It comprises the following tendencies:
- *Conservative* measures the extent of conscious concern for group norms or rules in order to reduce personal risk.
- *Pleasing* measures the need to seek approval of others in order to feel secure and worthwhile as a person.
- *Belonging* measures the need to conform and meet the expectations of those in positions of authority.
- *Passive* measures the degree to which one gives their power to others and to circumstances outside of their control.

Summary Measures

The following dimensions illustrate key relationships between the creative competencies and reactive tendencies.
- Reactive-Creative Scale reflects the balance between the creative and the reactive dimensions. The percentile score indicates the degree to which one's behavior arises from a creative or reactive orientation. It also suggests the degree to which self-concept and inner motivation is derived from external expectations, rules, norms, or conditions. Good balance results in high percentile scores.
- Relationship-Task Balance measures the degree of balance between achievement competencies and relationship competencies. Good balance results in high percentile scores.
- Leadership Potential Utilization is a summary measure taking in account all the competencies and tendencies.
- Leadership Effectiveness measures perceived effectiveness through a separate set of questions spread throughout the survey.

The Leadership Circle Profile of the TMI Research Group

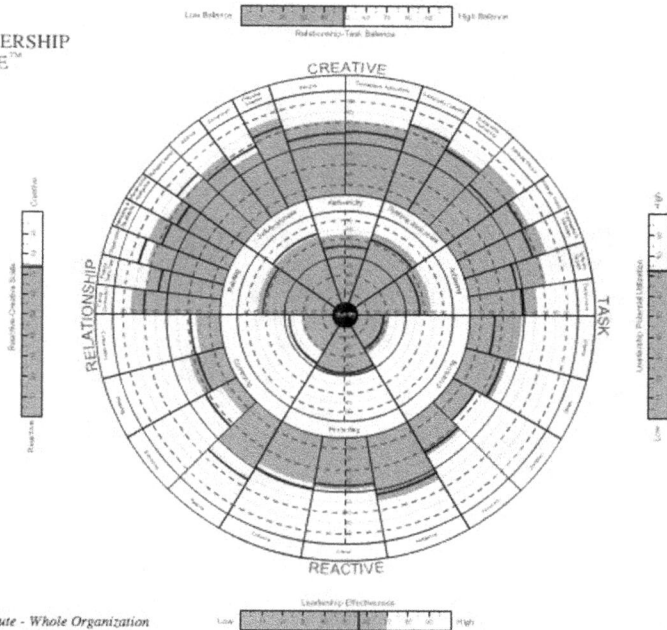

TMI The Monroe Institute - Whole Organization

© 2010 The Leadership Circle www.theleadershipcircle.com

Attachment 8

The Leadership Circle Profile of the University of Notre Dame Research Group

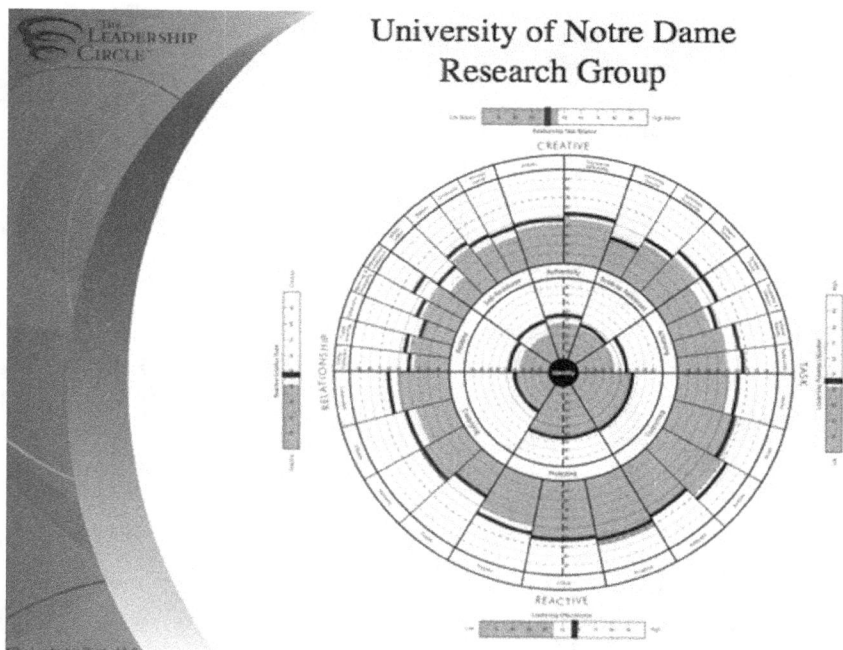

University of Notre Dame
Research Group

Attachment 9

The Leadership Circle Profile of Extraordinary Leader Research Group

Extraordinary Leader Research Group

Works Cited

A

Anderson, Robert. Founder and developer, The Leadership Circle Profile. Personal interview. 27 January 2009.

Argyris, Chris and Schön, Donald. *Theory in Practice: Increasing Professional Effectiveness.* San Francisco: Jossey-Bass. 1974.

Argyris, Chris. *Increasing Leadership Effectiveness.* New York: Wiley-Interscience. 1976.

Atwater, F. Holmes. *The Hemi-Sync Process.* The Monroe Institute, 2004.

B

Baldwin, Timothy & Danielson, Camden. "Formulating Learning Strategy in Organizations: Challenges Facing the Chief Learning Officer." *Academy of Management Annual Meeting.* Denver, CO: 2002.

- - - "Making Learning Strategy at the Top: Interviews with Ten of America's Chief Learning Officers." *Business Horizons.* Vol. 43, No. 6. November-December 2000.

Baldwin, Timothy; Danielson, Camden; and Wiggenhorn, William. "The Evolution of Learning Strategies in Organizations: From Employee Development to Business Redefinition." *Academy of Management Executive.* Vol. 11 No. 4. 1998.

Bedi, Ashok. "India: An Odyssey of Individuation of an Ancient Civilization." *Spring: A Journal of Archetype and Culture.* Vol. 90. Fall 2013.

Bennis, Warren. *On Becoming a Leader.* Reading, MA: Addison-Wesley Publishing, 1989.

Biblia Sacra Iuxta Vulgatam Clementinam, 4th ed. Alberto Colunga and Laurentio Turrado, eds. Matriti (Madrid): Editorial Católica, 1965.

Blake, William. *Selected Poems.* Ed. G. E. Bentley, Jr. London: Penguin Books, 2005.

C

Campbell, Joseph. *The Hero with a Thousand Faces*. Bollingen Series 17. Princeton, NJ: Second Edition: Princeton University Press, 1968.

- - - Interview by Bill Moyers. *The Power of Myth*. Ed. Betty Sue Flowers. New York: Broadway Books, 2001.

Cherman, Luiz. Personal interview. 10 September 2013.

Chesterton, G. K. *The Napoleon of Notting Hill*. London: Penguin Books, 1946.

Cicero, Marcus Tullius. *Basic Works of Cicero*. Ed. Moses Hadas. New York: Random House, 1951.

D

Danielson, Camden. *The Effects of Long-Term Participation in The Monroe Institute Programs – Part II*. www.monroeinstitute.org/research/program-benefits-study-2, 2010.

- - - "Different Thematic Approaches to the Study of Consciousness." *TMI Journal*, 2012 No.1.

Danielson, Camden & Wiggenhorn, William. "The Strategic Challenge for Learning Transfer: Chief Learning Officers Speak Out." *Improving Learning Transfer in Organizations*. Ed. Ed Holton and Tim Baldwin. San Francisco: Jossey-Bass, 2003.

Dostoevsky, Fyodor. *The Brothers Karamazov*. Trans. Richard Pevear and Larissa Volokhonsky. New York: Farrar, Straus and Giroux, 1990.

Dupuy, Francois. *The Customer's Victory*. Bloomington, IN: Indiana University Press, 1999.

E

Einstein, Albert. "Atomic Education Urged by Einstein." New York Times, May 25, 1946.

F

Frankfurt, Harry G. *The Reasons of Love*. Princeton, NJ: Princeton University Press, 2004.

Ferrer, Jorge. *Revisioning Transpersonal Theory: A Participatory Vision of Human Spirituality*. Albany, NY: State University of New York Press, 2001.

Forman, Robert K. C. *Mysticism, Mind, Consciousness*. Albany, NY: State University of New York Press, 1999.

Frazier, Ian. *On the Rez*. New York, NY: Picador USA, 2000.

G

Gallardo, Camilo. *The Mechanics of the Transcendent Function*. http://www.camilogallardo.com/index.php/resources1/the-mechanics-of-the-transcendent-function. 2005.

Gardner, Howard. *Multiple Intelligences*. New York: Basic Books, 2006.

Goethe, Johann Wolfgang Von. *Faust, Part Two*. Trans. Philip Wayne. London: Penguin Books, 1959.

Grof, Stanislav. *A Brief History of Transpersonal Psychology*. http://www.stanislavgrof.com/pdf/A%20Brief%20History%20of%20Transpersonal%20Psychology-Grof.pdf.

H

Handy, Charles. *The Age of Unreason*. Boston: Harvard Business School Press, 1989.

Hegel, G.W.F. *The Phenomenology of Mind*. Trans. J.B. Baillie. New York: Dover Philosophical Classics, 2003.

Heisenberg, Werner. *Physics and Philosophy: The Revolution in Modern Science*. New York: Harper & Row, 1958.

Hesse, Hermann. *Demian*. Trans. Michael Roloff and Michael Lebeck. New York: Harper Perennial Modern Classics, 1999.

Hillman, James. *Re-Visioning Psychology*. New York: HarperCollins Publishers. 1975.

Hock, Dee. *Birth of the Chaordic Age*. San Francisco: Berrett-Koehler Publishers, 1999.

Homer. *The Odyssey*. Trans. E.V. Rieu. Revised trans. D.C.H. Rieu. London: Penguin Group, 1991.

Horney, Karen. *Neurosis and Human Growth: The Struggle Towards Self-Realization*. New York: W.W. Norton & Co., 1950.

J

James, William. *The Varieties of Religious Experience: A Study in Human Nature*. New York: Routledge, 2008.

Jung, Carl Gustav. "Psychological Types." *The Collected Works of C.G. Jung*. Eds. & Trans. Gerhard Adler and R.F. C. Hull. Vol, 6. Bollingen Series XX. Princeton, NJ: Princeton University Press, 1971.

- - - "On the Psychology of the Unconscious." *The Collected Works of C.G. Jung*. Eds. & Trans. Gerhard Adler and R.F. C. Hull. Vol, 7. Bollingen Series XX. Princeton, NJ: Princeton University Press, 1953. 2nd ed. 1966.

- - - "The Transcendent Function." *The Collected Works of C.G. Jung*. Eds. & Trans. Gerhard Adler and R.F. C. Hull. Vol, 8. Bollingen Series XX. Princeton, NJ: Princeton University Press, 1960. 2nd ed. 1969.

- - - "Commentary on 'The Secret of the Golden Flower.'" *The Collected Works of C.G. Jung*. Eds. & Trans. Gerhard Adler and R.F. C. Hull. Vol, 13. Bollingen Series XX. Princeton, NJ: Princeton University Press, 1967.

- - - *Memories, Dreams, Reflections*. Ed. Aniela Jaffe. Trans. Richard and Clara Winston. New York: Vintage Books, 1989.

K

Kabat-Zinn, Jon. *Wherever You Go, There You Are*. New York: Hyperion Books. 1994.

Keats, John. *The Letters of John Keats*, 2nd ed. M.B. Forman, ed. London: Oxford University Press. 1935.

Kegan, Robert. *In Over our Heads: the Mental Demands of Modern Life*. Boston: Harvard University Press, 1994.

Kegan, Robert, and Lisa Laskow Lahey. *How the Way We Talk can Change the Way We Work*. San Francisco: Jossey-Bass, 2001.

- - - *Immunity to Change: How to Overcome It and Unlock the Potential in Yourself and Your Organization*. Boston: Harvard Business Press, 2009.

Kierkegaard, Søren. *Søren Kierkegaard's Journals and Papers*. Eds. & Trans. Howard V. and Edna H. Hong, assisted by Gregor Malantschuk. Index by N. Hong and C. Barker. 2nd ed. 7 vols. Bloomington: Indiana University Press, 1967-1978. 2nd ed. 1999.

Kuhn, Thomas S. *The Structure of Scientific Revolutions*. Second edition, enlarged. Chicago, IL: University of Chicago Press, 1970.

L

Lenoard, George. Mastery: *The Keys to Success and Long-term Fulfillment*. New York: Plume (Penguin Group), 1991.

- - - Personal interview. 22 February 1997.

M

Martin, Calvin Luther. *The Way of the Human Being*. New Haven, CT: Yale University Press, 1999.

Miller, Alice. *The Drama of the Gifted Child*. Trans. Ruth Ward. New York: Basic Books, Inc., 1981.

Milton, John. *Complete Poems and Major Prose*. Ed. Merritt Y. Hughes. New York: The Odyssey Press, 1957.

Monroe, Robert. *Journeys Out of the Body*. New York: A Dolphin Book, Doubleday, 1992.

- - - *Far Journeys*. New York: Doubleday, 1985.

Murphy, Michael. *The Future of the Body: Explorations Into the Further Evolution of Human Nature*. New York: Jeremy P. Tarcher/Putnam Books, 1992.

N

Newman, John Henry Cardinal. *Apologia Pro Vita Sua & Six Sermons*. Ed. Frank M. Turner. New Haven, CT: Yale University Press, 2008.
Nietzsche, Frederick. *Basic Writings of Nietzsche*. Trans. & Ed. Walter Kaufmann. New York: The Modern Library, 1992.

P

Peat, F. David. *Synchronicity: The Bridge Between Matter and Mind*. New York: Bantam Books. 1987.
Pieper, Josef. *Leisure the Basis of Culture*. trans. Alexandre Dru. San Francisco: Ignatius Press. 2009.
Pirsig, Robert. *Lila: An Inquiry into Morals*. New York: Bantam Books, 1991.
Plato. *The Collected Dialogues*. Eds. Edith Hamilton & Huntington Cairns. Bollingen Series LXXI. Princeton, NJ: Princeton University Press, 1961.

R

Rilke, Rainer Maria. *Letters to a Young Poet*, trans. Stephen Mitchell. New York: Vintage Books, 1986.
Rubin, Bruce Joel. "Jacob's Ladder." Mark Mixson, general editor, *The Applause Screenplay Series*. New York: Applause Theatre Book Publishers. 1990.
Russell, Ronald. *Journey of Robert Monroe: From Out of Body Explorer to Consciousness Pioneer*. Charlottesville, VA: Hampton Roads Publishing Company, 2007.
- - - Personal interview. 24 May 2012.

S

Schein, Edgar. *Organizational Culture and Leadership*, 2nd ed. San Francisco: Jossey-Bass. 1992.
Siegel, Daniel J. *Mindsight: The New Science of Personal Transformation*. New York: Bantam Books. 2001.

Shakespeare, William. *The Complete Works*. Ed. G.B. Harrison. New York: Harcourt, Brace & World, Inc., 1968.

Southern, R.W. *The Making of the Middle Ages*. New Haven, CT: Yale University Press, 1953.

T

Tarnas, Richard. *The Passion of the Western Mind: Understanding the Ideas that have Shaped Our World*. New York: Harmony Books, 1991.

Taylor, Jill Bolte. *Stroke of Insight*. TED.com. The Sapling Foundation, February 2008. Web. March 2008.

Tompkins, Teri C. and Rhodes, Kent. "Groupthink and the Ladder of Inference: Increasing Effective Decision Making." *The Journal of Human Resource and Adult Learning*, Vol. 8, Num. 2, December 2012.

Torbert, Bill and Associates. *Action Inquiry: The Secret of Timely and Transforming Leadership*. San Francisco: Berrett-Koehler, 2004.

W

Wilbur, Ken. *The Eye of Spirit: An Integral Vision for a World Gone Slightly Mad*. Boston: Shambhala Publications, Inc., 1997.

- - - *Sex, Ecology, Spirituality: The Spirit of Evolution*. Boston: Shambhala Publications. 1995.

Wilson, Colin. *The Outsider*. New York: Jeremy P. Tarcher/Putnam, 1982.

Wordsworth, William. *Selected Poems*. Ed. Walford Davies. London: J. M. Dent & Sons Ltd., 1975.

Y

Yeats, William Butler. *The Autobiography of William Butler Years*. New York: Collier Books, 1965.

www.ingramcontent.com/pod-product-compliance
Lightning Source LLC
Chambersburg PA
CBHW052127270326
41930CB00012B/2792